Betty Crocker's
COOKBOOK FOR
BOYS AND GIRLS

Golden Press • New York
Western Publishing Company, Inc.
Racine, Wisconsin

Director of Photography: Len Weiss

REVISED EDITION
with recipes selected from the original edition
Third Printing This Edition, 1985

Copyright © 1984, 1975 by General Mills, Inc., Minneapolis, Minnesota.

Printed in the U.S.A. by Western Publishing Company, Inc.
Published by Golden Press, New York, New York.
Library of Congress Catalog Card Number: 83-82255

Golden® and Golden Press® are trademarks of Western Publishing Company, Inc.
ISBN 0-307-09943-1

Contents

Cook's Corner

Kitchen Quiz

Can you put these kitchen terms where they belong?

Getting Ingredients Ready

CORE (lettuce, apple)

DRAIN (cooked macaroni)

GREASE (pan)

KNEAD (dough)

LIQUEFY (tomatoes)

MELT (chocolate)

PARE (potato)

PEEL (orange)

ROLL OUT (pastry)

SHRED (cabbage)

SNIP (parsley)

1 _____ Spread the bottom and sides of a pan with shortening.

2 _____ Change a solid food to a liquid by beating it, usually in the blender.

3 _____ Pour off liquid or let it run off through the holes in a sieve or colander.

4 _____ Cut off the skin.

5 _____ Flatten and spread with a rolling pin.

6 _____ Cut into thin pieces, using a knife or the large holes of a grater.

7 _____ Cut into very small pieces, using scissors.

8 _____ Change a solid food to a liquid by heating it.

9 _____ Pull off the skin.

10 _____ Curve your fingers and fold dough toward you, then push it away with the heels of your hands, using a quick rocking motion.

11 _____ Cut out the stem end or remove the seeds.

Mixing Ingredients

MIX (batter)

BEAT (eggs)

WHIP (cream)

FOLD (whipped cream)

TOSS (salad)

STIR (cookie dough)

1 _____ Tumble ingredients lightly with a lifting motion.

2 _____ Mix gently, bringing a rubber scraper down through a mixture, across the bottom, up and over the top until blended.

3 _____ Mix with a circular or figure-8 motion, using a spoon or fork.

4 _____ Combine to distribute ingredients evenly, using an electric mixer, blender or spoon.

5 _____ To make smooth with a vigorous over-and-over motion, using a spoon, whip or egg beater.

6 _____ Beat rapidly to make light and fluffy, using an electric mixer or egg beater.

(Clue: These are numbered from the gentlest action to the most vigorous.)

Cooking

BAKE (cake)

BOIL (water)

BOIL RAPIDLY (jelly)

BROWN (meat)

FRY (potatoes)

SCALD (milk)

SIMMER (soup)

DOT (casserole)

GARNISH (salad)

COOL (cookies)

REFRIGERATE (pudding)

1 _____ Cook in enough fat to cover the bottom of a pan.

2 _____ Heat milk until just below the boiling point so a skin forms on top.

3 _____ Allow to come down to room temperature.

4 _____ Heat until bubbles keep rising and breaking on the surface of a liquid.

5 _____ Place in the refrigerator.

6 _____ Decorate with pieces of colorful food.

7 _____ Cook in the oven.

8 _____ Heat until bubbles form rapidly and break on the surface of a liquid.

9 _____ Drop bits of butter or cheese here and there over a food.

10 _____ Heat liquid until just below the boiling point; bubbles form slowly and collapse *below* the surface.

11 _____ Cook on each side until a food changes color, usually in a small amount of fat over medium heat.

Answers

Getting Ingredients Ready
1. Grease; 2. Liquefy; 3. Drain; 4. Pare; 5. Roll out; 6. Shred; 7. Snip; 8. Melt; 9. Peel; 10. Knead; 11. Core.

Mixing Ingredients
1. Toss; 2. Fold; 3. Stir; 4. Mix; 5. Beat; 6. Whip.

Cooking
1. Fry; 2. Scald; 3. Cool; 4. Boil; 5. Refrigerate; 6. Garnish; 7. Bake; 8. Boil rapidly; 9. Dot; 10. Simmer; 11. Brown.

Utensils You Should Have

Apple corer

Long serrated knife

Sharp knife

Custard cups
(6- and 10-ounce)

Mixing bowls (set of 3)

Kitchen scissors

Can opener

Ice-cream scoop

Vegetable parer

Cookie cutter

Biscuit cutter

Potato masher

Vegetable brush

For Preparation

Timer

Egg beater

Pastry brush

Strainer

Covered rolling pin
and board

Colander

Cutting board

Melon baller

Ruler

For Measuring

Liquid measuring cup (1-cup)

Dry measuring cups
(1-, ½-, ⅓- and ¼-cup)

Rubber scraper

Spatula

Measuring spoons
(¼-, ½- and 1-teaspoon
and 1-tablespoon)

Long-handled fork

Wooden spoon or long-handled spoon with heatproof handle

Slotted spoon

Tongs

Double boiler

Saucepans with covers (2½- to 3-, 2- and 1-quart)

For Top-of-Range Cooking

Pancake turner

Griddle

Dutch oven with cover

Heavy skillets (8- and 10-inch)

Oblong baking pan, 13x9x2 inches

Muffin pan (6-cup)

Jelly roll pan, 15½x10½x1 inch

Square baking dish, 8x8x2 inches

Wire cooling rack

For Baking

Round layer cake pan, 8x1½ inches

Square baking pans, 8x8x2 and 9x9x2 inches

Loaf pan, 9x5x3 inches

Pie plate (9-inch)

Skewer (8-inch)

Cookie sheet

Pot holder

Casseroles with covers

Kitchen Math

3 teaspoons = 1 tablespoon
4 tablespoons = ¼ cup
5 tablespoons plus 1 teaspoon = ⅓ cup
8 tablespoons = ½ cup
16 tablespoons = 1 cup
2 cups = 1 pint
4 cups = 1 quart
2 quarts = ½ gallon

Butter or Margarine

4 sticks (1 pound) = 2 cups
1 stick (¼ pound) = ½ cup
½ stick (⅛ pound) = ¼ cup

Baking dishes are glass; baking pans are metal. Use shiny metal pans to make biscuits, muffins, cakes, cookies and yeast rolls a light brown. Use glass and dull metal pans for pies, breads and hot dishes. Follow the manufacturer's directions for pans with a non-stick coating.

Using Appliances

The Oven

- Arrange the shelves before you turn on the oven.
- Allow plenty of air space around each thing you're baking—no containers should touch.
- Alternate foods on each shelf so that one isn't directly over another.
- Use a tight-fitting cover or aluminum foil when the recipe calls for covering.
- Close the oven door quickly so heat won't be lost.

The Range

- Put large pans on large burners and small pans on small burners. Turn the handles so they don't stick out over the edge of the range, and make sure they're not over another burner either.

The Microwave Oven

- Read the instruction booklet to find out the kinds of foods your oven can handle and the correct cooking times.
- Cover most foods to prevent spattering.
- Allow a few minutes' standing time after cooking foods, since they keep on cooking when you take them out of the oven.
- Be careful not to burn yourself. Microwaves go right through containers without heating them, but the food may make them hot.
- See pages 19 and 53 for recipes with microwave instructions.

How to Measure

All-purpose flour: Dip from canister with dry measuring cup. Level with spatula.

Granulated sugar: Measure like flour.

Powdered sugar: Spoon lightly into dry measuring cup. Level with spatula. To remove lumps, press through sieve.

Brown sugar: Pack firmly into dry measuring cup. Level with spatula.

Buttermilk baking mix: Spoon lightly into dry measuring cup over waxed paper. Level with spatula. Baking mix will be lumpy. Pour excess from paper back into box.

Baking powder (and baking soda, cream of tartar, salt, spices): Dip and fill measuring spoon. Level with spatula.

Shredded cheese (and soft crumbs, shredded coconut, raisins, shelled nuts): Pack lightly into dry measuring cup until level.

Soft shortening: Pack firmly into dry measuring cup. Level with spatula and remove with rubber scraper.

Butter or margarine: Unwrap and cut, then soften at room temperature. (Use regular margarine bought in sticks.)

Molasses (and corn syrup): Pour into liquid measuring cup. Remove with rubber scraper.

Vanilla: Pour into measuring spoon held over custard cup or small bowl to catch any overflow.

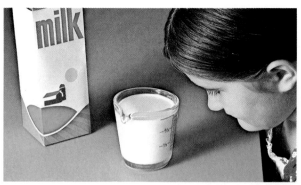

Milk (and other liquids): Set liquid measuring cup on counter, pour in liquid and bend down to check the correct amount at eye level.

Play It Safe!

1 Before you use a sharp knife, can opener, broiler, blender, mixer or microwave oven, be sure someone older is in the kitchen to help you.

2 Ask someone older to drain foods cooked in lots of hot water (like macaroni and spaghetti). If it isn't done just right, the steam could cause a burn.

3 Turn the handles of saucepans on the range away from you so they won't catch on anything and tip over (and be sure they're not over another burner).

4 Dry your hands after you wash them to avoid slippery fingers and shocks from electrical outlets.

5 Wipe up spills right away to avoid slippery floors.

6 Always turn the sharp edge of a knife or vegetable parer away from you and your hand when you chop or pare foods.

7 To avoid burns, use thick, dry pot holders, not thin ones or wet ones.

8 Turn off the blender or mixer before you scrape the side of the container or bowl so the scraper won't get caught in the blades.

9 Turn off the mixer and be sure it's unplugged whenever you put the beaters in or take them out.

10 Never disconnect an appliance by pulling the cord. Pull the plug instead.

Cook's Checklist

☐ Check with the grown-ups in your family for a convenient time to make a recipe.

☐ Wash your hands and wear an apron. Tie back your hair if it's long.

☐ Get out a tray, measuring cups and spoons and a spatula for leveling the ingredients you measure.

☐ Read the recipe all the way through.

☐ Get out all the ingredients and utensils listed in the recipe. Put them on the tray. Then when the tray is empty, you'll know you haven't left out any ingredients.

☐ Clean up as you go along. As you finish using a utensil, put it in warm, soapy water to soak. Oops! Don't put the knives in! When you wash them, be careful of those sharp blades.

☐ Rinse dishes that have had eggs, milk or mashed potatoes in them in cold water first, then in warm water.

☐ Finish washing and drying your utensils and put them away. Wash the counters and leave the kitchen clean and neat.

☐ Check the range to be sure the oven and surface units are turned off and wiped clean.

☐ Cook's reward: delicious results!

Table Talk

A nice-looking table makes mealtime more fun. Correct table setting means:

1 Dinner plate in center, 1 inch from edge of table.

2 Knife to right of plate, blade toward plate.

3 Spoon to right of knife.

4 Fork(s) to left of plate, tines up.

5 Water glass directly above point of knife.

6 Cup and saucer to right of spoon.

7 Salad plate to left of fork(s).

8 Napkin to left of fork(s) with the open corner toward you.

When you're out and in doubt—work from the outside in. Forks and spoons are placed with the piece to be used first on the outside.

But more important than which fork you use and how you hold it is *you*. Wash up before you go to the table . . . sit up straight . . . ask for what you want instead of reaching . . . remember to say "please" and "thank you" . . . take reasonable portions and small bites . . . butter your bread or roll one bite-size portion at a time . . . spoon your soup in the direction of boats sailing away from you . . . ask to be excused when you're finished eating.

Remember that good manners means being thoughtful of others. So wear a smile when you come to the table and try to make mealtime a pleasant time for everyone in your family—that way you'll enjoy it too!

Pictured: Quick-Energy Pickups (page 24), Apple-Cheese Snack (page 16) and Tomato Mush (page 16)

Raw Vegetable Snacks

Prepare any of the snacks below, then keep them fresh and crisp in a bowl of ice water in the refrigerator. Nibble anytime!

Carrot Curls: Wash and pare some carrots. Make long paper-thin curls by slicing the length of each carrot with a vegetable parer. (Always cut away from your hand!) Roll each slice around your finger, then poke a wooden pick through the carrot curl. Place in ice water in the refrigerator about 1 hour so the curls will hold their shape, then remove the wooden picks.

Celery Curls: Wash some celery stalks and pinch off the leaves. Cut several stalks at a time into 2- or 3-inch lengths on a cutting board. Cut the ends of each length into narrow strips (like fringe). Place in ice water in the refrigerator about 1 hour so the ends will curl.

Radish Fans: Wash and trim some radishes. Make thin parallel cuts in one side of each radish to about ¼ inch from the other side. Place in ice water in the refrigerator about 1 hour so the cuts will open to make a pretty fan.

Zucchini Sticks: Wash a zucchini and cut into short narrow sticks.

Cucumber Sticks: Wash and pare a cucumber and cut into short narrow sticks.

Cauliflowerets: Wash a head of cauliflower under running cold water, then break or cut into bite-size pieces.

Broccoli Buds: Wash some broccoli, then break or cut the buds into bite-size pieces.

Tomato Mush

Pictured on page 15.

3 drinks.

Utensils	Ingredients
Vegetable parer	1 small carrot
Sharp knife	½ celery stalk
Cutting board	¼ teaspoon salt
Blender	1 teaspoon paprika
	3 ice cubes
	⅔ cup tomato juice

1 Wash and pare 1 carrot. Wash ½ celery stalk and pinch off leaves.

2 Cut the carrot into 1-inch slices and the celery into 1-inch pieces on cutting board. Place in blender container.

3 Add ¼ teaspoon salt, 1 teaspoon paprika, 3 ice cubes and ⅔ cup tomato juice. Cover and blend on high speed 20 seconds. Serve right away.

Apple-Cheese Snack

Pictured on page 15.

1 snack.

Utensils	Ingredients
Apple corer	1 red or yellow apple
Cutting board	Small chunk of your
Sharp knife	favorite cheese (Cheddar, American, Swiss)
Small plate	

1 Wash and core 1 apple. Cut into quarters on cutting board, then cut each quarter into 4 or 5 slices. Arrange in circle on plate.

2 Cut the cheese into wedges and put them in the center of the plate. Munch and crunch!

Banana Boats

4 boats.

Utensils	Ingredients
Cutting board	¼ cup salted peanuts
Sharp knife	4 large bananas
Kitchen scissors	1 carton (4 ounces)
Small bowl	frozen whipped
Teaspoon	topping, thawed
Rubber scraper	4 maraschino cherries

1 Chop ¼ cup peanuts on cutting board.

2 Gently wash 4 bananas. Carefully slit top of each banana peel lengthwise, leaving about 1 inch uncut at each end. Cut away about ½ inch of the peel on each side of the slit with scissors.

3 Empty the whipped topping into bowl. Scoop out each banana in small pieces with teaspoon into the bowl. Save the banana peel shells. Fold the banana pieces into the topping with rubber scraper.

4 Fill each banana peel shell with ¼ of the banana-topping mixture. Sprinkle with ¼ of the chopped peanuts and top with 1 maraschino cherry.

5 Serve Banana Boats right away or refrigerate as long as 1 hour.

Slit the banana peel, then cut away about ½ inch of the peel on each side of the slit with scissors.

Fold the banana pieces into the whipped topping, then fill the shells with the mixture.

Scoop out small chunks of banana with a teaspoon. Save the banana peel shells to fill later.

Sprinkle each boat with chopped peanuts and top with a maraschino cherry.

Banana-Orange Junior

3 drinks.

Utensils	Ingredients
Blender	½ cup milk
Ice-cream scoop or	½ cup orange juice
large spoon	2 cups orange sherbet
3 tall glasses	1 banana

1 Pour ½ cup milk and ½ cup orange juice into blender container. Scoop in 1 cup of the sherbet. Peel 1 banana and break it into pieces into the container.

2 Cover and blend on high speed 10 seconds. Pour into 3 glasses. Top each with a scoop of sherbet from the remaining 1 cup. Serve right away.

Rainbow Float

1 float.

Utensils	Ingredients
Tall glass	Red fruit punch drink or
Ice-cream scoop or	fruit juice
large spoon	⅔ cup lemon sherbet
	Chilled carbonated
	lemon-lime soda pop
	or club soda

1 Fill glass halfway to the top with fruit punch drink. Scoop in ⅔ cup sherbet.

2 Fill the glass with soda pop. Serve the float right away.

Purple Cow Shakes

3 or 4 shakes.

Utensils	Ingredients
Blender	1 can (6 ounces) frozen
Ice-cream scoop or	grape juice
large spoon	concentrate
	1 cup milk
	2 cups vanilla ice cream

1 Pour the juice concentrate and 1 cup milk into blender container.

2 Scoop in 2 cups ice cream.

3 Cover and blend on high speed 30 seconds. Serve right away.

Note: No blender? Scoop the ice cream into a 2-quart jar with remaining ingredients. Cover tightly and shake. Or beat in a large bowl with an egg beater.

Cook's Corner

You need at least 3 glasses of milk a day to keep your bones and teeth healthy. Another way to get those good-for-you nutrients is to have 2 slices of cheese or 1 cup of cocoa or 1 malt instead of 1 glass of milk.

Here's a milk shake for breakfast time or anytime: Pour 1 cup milk into the blender container. Add 1 envelope (about 1.2 ounces) strawberry- or vanilla- or chocolate-flavored instant breakfast drink mix. Add ¼ cup canned crushed pineapple or 6 canned apricot halves or 1 small banana, peeled and sliced. Cover the container and blend on high speed 5 to 10 seconds or until smooth. Serve right away.

Cocoa

9 servings.

Utensils	Ingredients
Large saucepan	⅓ cup sugar
Long-handled spoon	⅓ cup cocoa
Egg beater (if you like)	¼ teaspoon salt
	1½ cups water
	4½ cups milk
	¼ teaspoon vanilla

1 Mix ⅓ cup sugar, ⅓ cup cocoa and ¼ teaspoon salt in saucepan. Add 1½ cups water. Heat to boiling, stirring constantly. Boil and stir 2 minutes.

2 Stir in 4½ cups milk. Heat through but do not boil. Add ¼ teaspoon vanilla.

3 Just before serving, beat until foamy or stir until smooth.

Note: The quickest way to make cocoa is with a microwave oven if you have one. Pour chocolate milk to within ½ inch of the top of a mug or cup. Cook uncovered (1 cup at a time) in microwave oven 1 minute 30 seconds or until hot. Place a marshmallow on top of the cocoa and sprinkle with a little cinnamon. Cook 20 seconds longer (if you heat more than 1 cup of cocoa, the cooking time will be longer).

Big Fat Cookies

Pictured on page 73.

About 30 cookies.

Utensils	Ingredients
Cookie sheet	1 package (18.5 ounces)
Large mixer bowl	yellow or devils food
Electric mixer	cake mix with pudding
Rubber scraper	½ cup water
Tablespoon	2 eggs
Pancake turner	1 cup semisweet
Wire cooling rack	chocolate chips

1 Heat oven to 375°. Grease cookie sheet with shortening.

2 Prepare the cake mix as directed on package except—use ½ cup water and 2 eggs. Omit salad oil. Drop the dough by rounded tablespoonfuls 3 inches apart onto the greased cookie sheet. Sprinkle with 1 cup chocolate chips.

3 Bake in 375° oven 8 to 10 minutes or until almost no impression remains when a cookie is touched lightly. Cool on cookie sheet 1 minute, then lift the cookies to rack with pancake turner.

VARIATION

Gumdrop Cookies: Follow recipe for Big Fat Cookies except—in place of the chocolate chips, use 1 cup small gumdrops. Cut the gumdrops in half so they won't sink to the bottom and stick.

Teddy Bear Paws

16 paws.

Utensils	Ingredients
Medium bowl	½ cup granulated sugar
Egg beater	¼ cup butter or mar-
Long-handled spoon	garine, softened
Breadboard and	(½ stick)
pastry cloth	2 tablespoons shortening
Rolling pin and	1 egg
stockinet cover	1 teaspoon vanilla
Custard cup	1¼ cups all-purpose
Cookie sheet	flour*
Table knife	½ teaspoon baking
Spatula	powder
Pancake turner	½ teaspoon salt
Wire cooling rack	About 3 tablespoons
	raspberry jam
	About 3 tablespoons
	chopped nuts
	About 3 tablespoons
	powdered sugar

1 Beat ½ cup granulated sugar, ¼ cup butter, 2 tablespoons shortening, 1 egg and 1 teaspoon vanilla in bowl. Stir in 1¼ cups flour, ½ teaspoon baking powder and ½ teaspoon salt and mix until smooth. Cover and refrigerate at least 1 hour.

2 Cover breadboard with pastry cloth, tucking ends underneath. Cover rolling pin with stockinet cover. For convenience, place some flour in custard cup. Sprinkle the covered board and rolling pin lightly with the flour and rub it in until it disappears.

3 Grease cookie sheet with shortening.

4 When the dough has been refrigerated at least 1 hour, heat oven to 400°.

5 Roll the dough into a 12-inch square on the covered board. Cut into 3-inch squares.

6 Spread about ½ teaspoon jam down the center of each square. Sprinkle the jam on each square with about ½ teaspoon nuts.

7 Fold one edge of the dough over the jam and nuts, then fold the other edge over the top. Lift the unbaked cookies onto the greased cookie sheet with pancake turner.

8 Make 4 or 5 cuts in one long side of each cookie and spread the cuts slightly apart. Sprinkle each cookie with about ½ teaspoon powdered sugar.

9 Bake in 400° oven 6 minutes or until light brown. Lift to rack with pancake turner.

* Do not use self-rising flour in this recipe.

VARIATIONS

Pinwheels: Follow recipe for Teddy Bear Paws except—cut unfolded 3-inch squares diagonally from each corner almost to the center. Fold every other point to the center to make pinwheel. Spoon ½ teaspoon jam onto the center of each pinwheel and sprinkle with ½ teaspoon chopped nuts and ½ teaspoon powdered sugar. Bake as directed.

Lollipops: Follow recipe for Teddy Bear Paws except—do not roll the dough. Drop by tea- spoonfuls onto ungreased cookie sheet. Flatten slightly with your fingers. Place 1 wooden ice-cream stick and 1 milk choco- late star on each circle. Top with another teaspoonful of dough and press the dough together with your fingers. Bake as directed about 8 minutes or until light brown.

Mexican Cookies: Follow recipe for Teddy Bear Paws except—in place of the vanilla, use 1 teaspoon anise extract. Cut the 12- inch square into 3-inch flower shapes with a cookie cutter. Sprinkle with colored sugar. Bake as directed.

Roll the cookie dough into a 12-inch square, then cut into 3-inch squares.

Spread jam down the center of each square, then sprinkle the jam with chopped nuts.

Fold one edge over, then fold the other edge over that. (The dough may crack a little bit.)

Make 4 or 5 cuts in one long side of each cookie and spread the cuts slightly apart.

Lollipops, Pinwheels, Teddy Bear Paws and Mexican Cookies

Chocolate Chip Cookies

About 24 cookies.

Utensils	Ingredients
Cookie sheet	¼ cup butter or margarine, softened (½ stick)
Large bowl	
Long-handled spoon	
Teaspoon	⅔ cup brown sugar (packed)
Pancake turner	1 egg
Wire cooling rack	1⅓ cups buttermilk baking mix
	¼ cup all-purpose flour
	1 package (6 ounces) semisweet chocolate chips

1 Heat oven to 375°. Grease cookie sheet with shortening.

2 Mix ¼ cup butter, ⅔ cup brown sugar and 1 egg in bowl. Stir in 1⅓ cups baking mix and ¼ cup flour and mix until smooth. Stir in the chocolate chips.

3 Drop the dough by rounded teaspoonfuls about 2 inches apart onto the greased cookie sheet.

4 Bake in 375° oven 8 to 10 minutes or until almost no impression remains when a cookie is touched lightly. Immediately lift the cookies to wire cooling rack with pancake turner.

VARIATION

Yo-Yo Cookies: Bake Chocolate Chip Cookies. When cool, put the flat sides of the baked cookies together in pairs, attaching them with your favorite frosting. Tuck the end of a 3-inch licorice string between each pair of cookies if you like.

Favorite Brownies

36 brownies.

Utensils	Ingredients
Oblong baking pan, 13 × 9 × 2 inches	4 ounces unsweetened chocolate
Pastry brush	⅔ cup shortening
Large saucepan	2 cups granulated sugar
Long-handled spoon	4 eggs
Rubber scraper	1 teaspoon vanilla
Wire cooling rack	1¼ cups all-purpose flour*
Table knife	1 teaspoon baking powder
	1 teaspoon salt
	1 cup chopped nuts
	Powdered sugar

1 Heat oven to 350°. Generously grease baking pan with shortening, using pastry brush.

2 Heat 4 ounces chocolate and ⅔ cup shortening in saucepan over low heat until the chocolate melts. Remove from heat. Mix in 2 cups granulated sugar, 4 eggs and 1 teaspoon vanilla. Stir in 1¼ cups flour, 1 teaspoon baking powder, 1 teaspoon salt and 1 cup chopped nuts. Spread the batter in the greased pan with rubber scraper.

3 Bake in 350° oven 30 minutes or until the brownies start to pull away from the sides of the pan. Do not overbake!

4 Cool the brownies slightly on rack. Cut into bars, about 2 inches long and 1½ inches wide. Cool completely. Sprinkle with powdered sugar.

* If using self-rising flour, omit the baking powder and salt.

Snickersnack

About 7 cups snack.

Utensils	Ingredients
Large bowl	4 cups toasted oat cereal
Spoon	1 can (6½ ounces) salted peanuts
Small saucepan	1 cup golden raisins
Fork	¼ cup butter or margarine (½ stick)
	1 package (6 ounces) semisweet chocolate chips

1 Mix 4 cups cereal, the peanuts and 1 cup raisins in bowl.

2 Melt ¼ cup butter in saucepan over low heat.

3 Pour the melted butter over the cereal mixture, using fork to toss lightly until mixture is coated. Sprinkle the chocolate chips over the mixture and toss again. Serve in bowls for nibbles or pack in small plastic bags for snacks or lunch box treats.

Cereal Sundae

1 sundae.

Utensils	Ingredients
Cereal bowl	Your favorite dry cereal
Ice-cream scoop or large spoon	Your favorite ice cream

Fill bowl halfway to the top with cereal. Place a large scoop of ice cream in the center. Sprinkle with a little more cereal. Serve right away.

Munchy Crunchy Granola

4 cups granola.

Utensils	Ingredients
Kitchen scissors	½ cup dried apples, apricots or mixed fruit
Jelly roll pan, 15½ × 10½ × 1 inch, or 2 oblong baking pans, 13 × 9 × 2 inches	1½ cups oats
	1 cup golden raisins
	1 package (4½ ounces) toasted sunflower nuts
Spoon	¼ cup sesame seeds
	¼ cup brown sugar (packed)
	¼ cup salad oil
	2 tablespoons vanilla
	¼ teaspoon salt

1 Heat oven to 350°.

2 Cut ½ cup dried apples into small pieces with scissors.

3 Spread the apple pieces and remaining ingredients in ungreased jelly roll pan. Mix well.

4 Bake in 350° oven 10 minutes. Remove from the oven and stir.

5 Return to the oven and bake 10 minutes more. Use the granola as a topping for cereal or ice cream, or serve in bowls for nibbles, or pack in small plastic bags for snacks or lunch box treats. Store any leftover granola tightly covered in refrigerator.

Quick-Energy Pickups

Pictured on page 15.

30 pickups.

Utensils	Ingredients
Waxed paper	3 or 4 square graham
Medium bowl	crackers
Spoon	1 cup powdered sugar
Teaspoon	1 cup crunchy peanut
Cookie sheet	butter
	1 cup semisweet
	chocolate chips
	½ cup instant nonfat
	dry milk
	3 tablespoons water

1 Crush 3 or 4 graham crackers with your fingers onto sheet of waxed paper.

2 Mix remaining ingredients thoroughly in bowl.

3 Shape teaspoonfuls of the mixture into 1-inch balls. Roll the balls in the graham cracker crumbs until coated.

4 Arrange the coated balls on ungreased cookie sheet and refrigerate about 20 minutes or until firm.

Note: In place of the graham crackers, you can use ½ cup prepared graham cracker crumbs or ⅔ cup flaked coconut.

Strawberry Squares

36 squares.

Utensils	Ingredients
Square baking pan,	½ cup butter or mar-
9 × 9 × 2 inches	garine (1 stick)
Large saucepan	3 cups miniature marsh-
Long-handled spoon	mallows or 32 large
Sharp knife	marshmallows
	½ cup instant nonfat
	dry milk
	½ cup strawberry-
	flavored quick milk
	mix
	4 cups toasted oat
	cereal
	1 cup flaked coconut

1 Grease baking pan with some butter or margarine.

2 Heat ½ cup butter, 3 cups miniature marshmallows, ½ cup dry milk and ½ cup milk mix in saucepan over low heat until smooth, stirring constantly. Remove from heat.

3 Stir in 4 cups cereal and 1 cup coconut until coated. Empty into the buttered pan. Rub a little butter on the back of the spoon and use it to pat the mixture evenly in the pan. Cool. Cut into 1½-inch squares.

Sweets give you quick energy, but be careful not to eat too many—that extra energy can turn into fat. So when you feel like having a snack, don't forget the milk, cereal, fruit and vegetable snacks in this chapter. They're a wonderful way to include the foods you need every day.

Pictured: Tacos Sealed with Refried Beans (page 34)

Mmm – Main Dishes

Lift the fried bologna slices into muffin cups and press down so they fit the cups.

Carefully break an egg into the center of each bologna cup to hold it down.

Loosen the baked bologna cups with a table knife and lift them from the muffin pan with a spoon.

Eggs in Bologna Cups

6 servings.

Utensils	Ingredients
Pastry brush	2 teaspoons shortening
Muffin pan	6 slices bologna, each
Large skillet	about 4 inches across
Tongs or pancake	6 eggs
turner	6 teaspoons milk
Table knife	Salt
Spoon	Pepper
Serving platter	Paprika

1 Heat oven to 375°.

2 Grease 6 muffin cups with some shortening, using pastry brush.

3 Melt 2 teaspoons shortening in skillet over low heat.

4 Place 3 slices bologna in the skillet and fry until the edges curl and the centers puff. Lift each slice with tongs into a muffin cup and press down so the slice fits the cup. Repeat with remaining bologna slices.

5 Break 1 egg into the center of each bologna slice to hold it down.

6 Pour 1 teaspoon milk over each egg. Sprinkle eggs lightly with salt, pepper and paprika.

7 Bake uncovered in 375° oven 15 to 20 minutes or until the eggs are set.

8 Loosen each bologna cup with knife and lift to platter with spoon.

Shake-Em-Up Scrambled Eggs

4 servings.

Utensils	Ingredients
Sharp knife	1 medium tomato
Cutting board	4 eggs
1-quart jar with cover	½ cup shredded Cheddar
Large skillet	cheese (about 2
Pancake turner	ounces)
	½ teaspoon salt
	Dash of pepper
	1 tablespoon shortening

1 Wash and cut stem end from 1 tomato. Chop the tomato into ½-inch pieces on cutting board. Place in jar.

2 Add 4 eggs, ½ cup shredded cheese, ½ teaspoon salt and dash of pepper to the chopped tomato. Cover the jar tightly and shake well.

3 Melt 1 tablespoon shortening in skillet over low heat. Tilt and turn the skillet to coat evenly with the melted shortening.

4 Pour the egg mixture into the hot skillet and cook over medium heat. Turn gently with pancake turner as the mixture starts to set at the bottom.

5 Cook until the eggs are cooked through but are still moist and shiny, 5 to 8 minutes.
Note: In place of the tomato, you can use 1 small celery stalk, chopped, or about ⅓ of a medium green pepper, chopped. Add ¼ cup milk.

This recipe can be doubled for families that love eggs. Use a 2-quart jar with cover to shake the eggs.

Fried Egg

1 egg.

Utensils	Ingredients
Small skillet	Butter, margarine or
Saucer	bacon drippings
Long-handled spoon	1 egg
Pancake turner (if you	Salt
like)	Pepper

1 Heat a thin layer of butter in skillet over medium-high heat. Break 1 egg into saucer and carefully slip the egg into the hot butter. Reduce heat.

2 Cook over low heat, spooning the butter over the egg, until the white is set and a film forms over the yolk. The egg is now cooked sunny-side up.

3 If you like, turn the egg over gently with pancake turner and cook a little more. Now the egg is cooked over easy. Sprinkle with salt and pepper before serving.

VARIATION

Poached-fried Egg: Follow recipe for Fried Egg except—cook the egg over low heat until the edge turns white. Add ½ teaspoon water and cover. Cook until the white is set and a film forms over the yolk.

Whenever you're cooking something on the range, it's smart to fit your pan size to the burner size—don't put a small pan on a great big burner! And for safety, turn pan handles so they don't stick out over the edge of the range, but make sure that they're not over another burner.

Glazed Chicken Drumsticks

About 14 drumsticks.

Utensils	Ingredients
Oblong baking dish, 13½ × 8¾ × 1¾ inches	3 pounds chicken drumsticks
Small bowl	3 tablespoons soy sauce
Fork	2 tablespoons honey
Aluminum foil	1 tablespoon salad oil
Broiler pan with rack	1 tablespoon chili sauce
Tongs	½ teaspoon salt
Pastry brush	¼ teaspoon ginger
Fork	⅛ teaspoon garlic powder

1 Place the drumsticks in ungreased baking dish.

2 Mix remaining ingredients in bowl with fork and pour over the drumsticks.

3 Cover the baking dish with aluminum foil and refrigerate at least 1 hour.

4 When the drumsticks have been refrigerated at least 1 hour, heat oven to 375°.

5 Lift the drumsticks with tongs onto rack in the broiler pan. Brush the drumsticks with the sauce remaining in the baking dish.

6 Bake in 375° oven 50 to 60 minutes or until the drumsticks are tender when pierced with fork.

Note: Many oven and broiler pans now have nonstick wipe-clean finishes. If your broiler pan isn't easy to clean, you may want to line it with aluminum foil.

Chicken-Fried Cubed Steaks

4 servings.

Utensils	Ingredients
Large skillet	2 tablespoons shortening
Tongs	½ package (4¾ ounces) seasoned coating mix for chicken (with shaker bag)
Pancake turner	
Serving platter	
Fork	4 beef cubed steaks (1½ to 2 pounds)
	¼ to ⅓ cup warm water

1 Melt 2 tablespoons shortening in skillet over low heat. While the shortening melts, measure 4 tablespoons of the coating mix into the shaker bag. (Rewrap remaining coating mix to use another time.) Shake 4 cubed steaks, one at a time, in the shaker bag until coated. (You'll use remaining coating mix in the shaker bag later.)

2 Place the coated steaks in the hot skillet with tongs. Increase heat to medium-high and fry the steaks about 5 minutes on each side. (You may want to ask for a second opinion in deciding when they are cooked through.)

3 Lift the steaks to platter with pancake turner. Shake the coating mix remaining in the shaker bag into the skillet. Add ¼ to ⅓ cup warm water and stir with fork to mix with the coating mix and meat scrapings. Heat to boiling. Stir the sauce and pour over the steaks.

Oven Cobblestone Stew

6 to 8 servings.

Utensils	Ingredients
Cutting board	2 pounds beef round steak or stew meat
Sharp knife	6 medium carrots
Vegetable parer	6 medium potatoes
Oblong baking pan, 13 × 9 × 2 inches	6 small onions
Fork	1 can (10¾ ounces) condensed cream of mushroom soup
Small bowl	
Spoon	1 envelope (about 1 ounce) brown gravy mix
Aluminum foil	
2 teaspoons	¼ cup water
	1 teaspoon horseradish
	½ teaspoon salt
	Cobblestone Biscuits (right)

1 Heat oven to 325°.

2 Cut the meat into 1-inch cubes on cutting board. Wash and pare 6 carrots and 6 potatoes and peel 6 onions. Cut each of the carrots and potatoes in half.

3 Mix the meat and vegetables in ungreased baking pan with fork and spread to the edges of the pan.

4 Pour the soup into bowl. Stir in remaining ingredients except Cobblestone Biscuits and pour over the meat and vegetables in the pan. Cover tightly with aluminum foil.

5 Bake in 325° oven 3 hours.

6 While the stew is baking, mix the dough for Cobblestone Biscuits and refrigerate it.

7 Carefully remove the stew from oven. Increase oven temperature to 450°.

8 Drop teaspoonfuls of the biscuit dough about ½ inch apart onto the stew. (Use 2 teaspoons, one to push the dough from the other. Work as fast as you can.)

9 Bake about 10 minutes or until the biscuits are golden brown.

Cobblestone Biscuits

Utensils	Ingredients
Medium bowl	1 cup buttermilk baking mix
Fork	½ cup grated American cheese food
	¼ cup cold water
	2 tablespoons mayonnaise or salad dressing

Mix all ingredients to a soft dough in bowl with fork. Now continue with Step 6.

Growing boys and girls need 2 or more servings of meat every day. (You can substitute fish, poultry, cheese or eggs for a serving of meat if you like.) These protein-rich foods help make muscles and help you grow and stay strong.

No-Crust Wide-Eyed Pizzas

4 pizzas.

Utensils	Ingredients
Medium bowl	1 can (8 ounces) tomato sauce
Fork	1 pound ground beef
Jelly roll pan, 15½ × 10½ × 1 inch	½ cup packaged dry bread crumbs
Rubber scraper	½ teaspoon salt
Cutting board	½ teaspoon oregano
Sharp knife	2 pimiento-stuffed or pitted black olives
	½ cup shredded mozzarella cheese (about 2 ounces)
	½ cup shredded Cheddar cheese (about 2 ounces)
	4 slices canned pimiento

1 Heat oven to 425°.

2 Measure out ½ cup of the tomato sauce. (You'll also use the sauce remaining in the can, so keep it handy.)

3 Mix the ground beef, ½ cup bread crumbs, the ½ cup tomato sauce, ½ teaspoon salt and ½ teaspoon oregano in bowl with fork.

4 Divide the ground beef mixture into 4 equal parts. Place the parts several inches apart in ungreased jelly roll pan. Pat each into a 4½-inch circle about ½ inch thick. Pinch the edge of each circle to make a little stand-up rim.

5 Pour about 2 tablespoons of the remaining tomato sauce into the center of each circle and spread it to the edge with rubber scraper.

6 Bake in 425° oven 15 to 20 minutes. (Ask someone else to help you decide when the pizzas are done if you're not sure.)

7 While the pizzas are baking, cut 2 olives crosswise into 4 slices each on cutting board.

8 Remove the pan from oven and turn off oven. Sprinkle each pizza with about 2 tablespoons shredded mozzarella cheese for a face and about 2 tablespoons shredded Cheddar cheese around the edge for hair. Use the olive and pimiento slices to make the eyes and mouth. Return the pizzas to warm oven and heat about 5 minutes or until the cheese melts.

Cook's Corner

What you eat makes you what you are. Most foods contain many hidden helpers called nutrients—magical substances that keep you healthy, help you grow and keep your body in good repair. To stay full of pep, try at least a little of every kind of food served at your table. A good variety of meats, fruits and vegetables, dairy foods and cereal foods will give a shine to your hair, a sparkle to your smile and a bounce to your step.

Juicy Hamburgers

6 hamburgers.

Utensils	Ingredients
Medium bowl	1½ pounds ground beef
Fork	¼ cup water
Large skillet or baking pan with rack	3 to 4 teaspoons instant minced onion* or ¼ cup frozen chopped onion
	1 teaspoon salt
	1 teaspoon Worcestershire sauce
	¼ teaspoon pepper

1 Mix all ingredients in bowl with fork.

2 Shape the mixture with your hands into 6 patties about ¾ inch thick.

3 Cook in one of the following ways:
To panfry: Fry the patties in skillet over medium heat 5 minutes on each side. (Ask someone to help you decide when the patties are done if you're not sure.)
To oven-bake: Heat oven to 350°. Place the patties on rack in baking pan. Bake in 350° oven 20 minutes. (Ask someone to help you decide when the patties are done if you're not sure.)
*Before adding instant minced onion, soak in an equal amount of water 3 to 4 minutes.

Sloppy Joes

6 to 8 sandwiches.

Utensils	Ingredients
Cutting board	1 celery stalk
Sharp knife	1 pound ground beef
Large skillet	3 tablespoons instant minced onion
Long-handled spoon	1 teaspoon salt
Cookie sheet	⅛ teaspoon pepper
Pancake turner	1 jar (about 16 ounces) spaghetti sauce
Serving platter	6 to 8 hamburger buns

1 Wash 1 celery stalk and pinch off leaves. Chop the celery into ½-inch pieces on cutting board.

2 Crumble the ground beef into skillet. Cook and stir over medium-high heat until brown on all sides, about 10 minutes. Spoon out any fat and throw it away.

3 Stir the celery, 3 tablespoons minced onion, 1 teaspoon salt, ⅛ teaspoon pepper and the spaghetti sauce into the ground beef. Heat to boiling, stirring constantly. Reduce heat. Simmer uncovered over low heat 10 minutes, stirring occasionally.

4 Cut 6 to 8 hamburger buns crosswise in half and place cut sides up on ungreased cookie sheet. Adjust broiler rack so the tops of the buns will be 4 to 5 inches from heat. Set oven control at broil and/or 550°.

5 Toast the buns until light brown. Watch carefully—it will take just 1 or 2 minutes. Lift the buns to platter with pancake turner. Spoon the ground beef mixture onto bottom half of each bun and cover with top half.

Bumpy Meatballs

4 servings.

Utensils	Ingredients
Medium bowl	1½ pounds ground beef
Fork	½ cup uncooked regular rice
Large skillet	¼ cup water
Slotted spoon	1 tablespoon instant minced onion*
1½-quart casserole with cover	1 teaspoon salt
Small bowl	1 teaspoon Worcestershire sauce
Spoon	¼ teaspoon pepper
	1 can (11 ounces) condensed Cheddar cheese soup
	¼ cup milk
	Paprika

1 Heat oven to 350°.

2 Mix all ingredients except the soup, milk and paprika in medium bowl with fork. Shape the mixture with your hands into 20 meatballs about the size of golf balls.

3 Brown several meatballs at a time in skillet over medium-high heat. As the meatballs brown, lift them with slotted spoon to ungreased casserole and add more meatballs to the skillet.

4 Mix the soup and ¼ cup milk in small bowl until smooth. Pour over the browned meatballs in the casserole. Sprinkle with paprika.

5 Bake in 350° oven 1 hour to 1 hour and 15 minutes or until the rice is tender.

* Before adding instant minced onion, soak in an equal amount of water 3 to 4 minutes.

One-Pot Italian Spaghetti

4 to 6 servings.

Utensils	Ingredients
Dutch oven with cover	1 pound ground beef
Long-handled spoon	2 tablespoons instant minced onion or ⅓ cup frozen chopped onion
	1 can (8 ounces) tomato sauce
	1 can (15 ounces) spaghetti sauce with mushrooms
	1½ teaspoons salt
	1 teaspoon sugar
	2 cups water
	1 package (about 7 ounces) long spaghetti
	3 tablespoons grated Parmesan cheese (if you like)

1 Crumble the ground beef into Dutch oven. Cook and stir over medium-high heat until brown on all sides, about 10 minutes. Spoon out any fat and throw it away.

2 Stir 2 tablespoons minced onion, the tomato sauce and spaghetti sauce into the ground beef. Add 1½ teaspoons salt, 1 teaspoon sugar, 2 cups water and the spaghetti (uncooked). Heat to boiling over medium-high heat, stirring occasionally to prevent sticking.

3 Reduce heat. Cover and simmer over low heat about 15 minutes or until the spaghetti is tender. Remove from heat and stir once. Sprinkle with 3 tablespoons grated cheese just before serving.

Tacos Sealed
with Refried Beans

Pictured on page 25.

10 tacos.

Utensils	Ingredients
Cutting board	Lettuce wedge (about
Sharp knife	1 inch thick)
3 small serving bowls	1 large tomato
Large skillet	1 package (4 ounces)
Long-handled spoon	shredded Cheddar
Cookie sheet	cheese (about 1 cup)
Pancake turner	1 pound ground beef
Serving platter	3 tablespoons instant
Large serving bowl	minced onion or
	½ cup frozen chopped
	onion
	1 can (15 ounces)
	tomato sauce
	1 teaspoon garlic salt
	1 teaspoon chili powder
	Dash of pepper
	Refried Beans (right)
	1 package (about 4
	ounces) taco shells
	(10 shells)
	Bottled taco sauce

1 Chop the lettuce into long shreds on cutting board. Place the lettuce in small serving bowl.

2 Wash and cut stem end from 1 tomato. Chop into ¼-inch pieces. Place in another small serving bowl. Empty the shredded cheese into another small serving bowl.

3 Heat oven to temperature given on taco shell package.

4 Crumble the ground beef into skillet. Cook and stir over medium-high heat until brown on all sides, about 10 minutes. Spoon out any fat and throw it away.

5 Stir 3 tablespoons minced onion, the tomato sauce, 1 teaspoon garlic salt, 1 teaspoon chili powder and dash of pepper into the ground beef. Reduce heat. Simmer uncovered over low heat 15 minutes, stirring occasionally.

6 While the ground beef mixture is simmering, prepare Refried Beans and heat the taco shells as directed on package. Lift the taco shells to platter with pancake turner.

7 Pour the ground beef mixture into large serving bowl. Serve along with the tacos, lettuce, tomato and cheese. Let each person make his or her own taco combination, sealing the taco by spreading the opening with the Refried Beans. Pass taco sauce.

Refried Beans

Utensils	Ingredients
Large saucepan	2 cans (about 16
Long-handled spoon	ounces each) hot
Small serving bowl	chili beans or baked
	beans
	¼ teaspoon chili powder
	¼ teaspoon onion salt
	Dash of garlic salt

Drain liquid from the cans of chili beans into saucepan. Stir in ¼ teaspoon chili powder, ¼ teaspoon onion salt and dash of garlic salt. Cook over low heat 5 minutes. Stir in the beans. Increase heat to medium and cook until the beans are dry, about 20 minutes, stirring frequently. Pour into serving bowl. Now continue with Step 6.

Basic Meat Loaf

8 to 10 servings.

Utensils	Ingredients
Large bowl	1 egg
Large fork	½ cup milk
Table knife	¾ cup quick-cooking
Oblong baking pan,	oats
13 × 9 × 2 inches	3 teaspoons salt
	1 teaspoon instant beef
	bouillon
	3 tablespoons instant
	minced onion* or
	½ cup frozen chopped
	onion
	2 teaspoons horseradish
	2½ pounds lean ground
	beef

1 Heat oven to 350°.

2 Mix all ingredients in bowl with fork. (This will take some mixing! Cutting through several times with knife will help.)

3 Place the ground beef mixture in ungreased baking pan. Shape with your hands into a loaf about 9 inches long, 5 inches wide and 3 inches thick.

4 Bake in 350° oven uncovered 1 hour and 30 minutes or until crusty and brown.
* Before adding instant minced onion, soak in an equal amount of water 3 to 4 minutes.

VARIATIONS

Zingy Horseradish Meat Loaf: Follow recipe for Basic Meat Loaf except—before baking, spread ¼ cup horseradish over the top of the loaf.

Barbecue Meat Loaf: Follow recipe for Basic Meat Loaf except—before baking, spread ¼ cup barbecue sauce over the top of the loaf.

Cheesy Meat Loaf: Follow recipe for Basic Meat Loaf except—after baking, overlap three 4-inch-square cheese slices on the top of the loaf. The heat from the loaf will melt the cheese.

Flowerpot Meat Loaf: Follow recipe for Basic Meat Loaf except—after baking, make a flower design, using a ring of sliced pimiento-stuffed olives for the flower petals; a cherry tomato for the center of the flower; green pepper strips for the stem, leaves and flowerpot and celery leaves for grass.

Football Meat Loaf: Follow recipe for Basic Meat Loaf except—before baking, shape the meat mixture into an oval that looks like a football, about 8 inches long and 5 inches wide at the middle. After baking, arrange strips of canned sliced pimiento (drained) on top to look like the lacings of a football. If you like, serve on a bed of spinach: Cook three 10-ounce packages frozen spinach as directed on packages. Drain spinach and arrange around football. (You don't like spinach? Try it—you might be surprised!)

Sticky Barbecued Ribs

5 or 6 servings.

Utensils	Ingredients
Cutting board	1 large onion
Sharp knife	1 cup catsup
Medium saucepan	¼ cup vinegar
Long-handled spoon	3 tablespoons brown
Dutch oven with cover	sugar
Tongs	2 tablespoons flour
Waxed paper	1 teaspoon salt
Deep platter or soup	1 teaspoon paprika
tureen	½ teaspoon curry
	powder
	½ teaspoon dry mustard
	¼ teaspoon chili powder
	1 can (10½ ounces)
	condensed consommé
	3 pounds fresh pork
	spareribs

1 Peel 1 onion and ask someone older to help you slice it on cutting board. (Those onions do slip around!)

2 Empty 1 cup catsup, ¼ cup vinegar, 3 tablespoons brown sugar, 2 tablespoons flour, 1 teaspoon salt, 1 teaspoon paprika, ½ teaspoon curry powder, ½ teaspoon dry mustard and ¼ teaspoon chili powder into saucepan. Stir in the consommé and onion slices. (You'll use this as a sauce later.)

3 Cut the spareribs into 6 pieces (try to make them about the same size).

4 Arrange oven racks so Dutch oven will fit on the lower rack. Heat oven to 350°.

5 Cook 3 pieces of ribs in Dutch oven over medium-high heat, turning with tongs to brown them on all sides. As the pieces brown, lift them with the tongs to waxed paper to make room for the other pieces. Once all the pieces are brown, place them meaty sides up in the Dutch oven.

6 Pour the seasoned consommé over the ribs. (Now you see why you used a saucepan —for easier pouring.)

7 Bake the ribs uncovered in 350° oven 1 hour and 15 minutes. Cover and bake 30 minutes. Lift the ribs with the tongs onto deep platter. Stir the sauce in the Dutch oven and pour it over the ribs.

Baked Pork Tenderloins

4 to 6 servings.

Utensils	Ingredients
Shallow roasting pan	2 pork tenderloins
with rack	(¾ pound each)
Small saucepan	1 jar (12 ounces) peach
Spoon	or apricot jam
Cutting board	1 teaspoon salt
Sharp knife	1 teaspoon dry mustard
	1 teaspoon soy sauce

1 Heat oven to 350°. Place the tenderloins on rack in the roasting pan.

2 Mix remaining ingredients in saucepan. Spoon about half of the sauce over the tenderloins.

3 Bake the tenderloins in 350° oven 1 hour and 30 minutes.

4 Heat remaining sauce in the saucepan over low heat. Ask someone older to slice the tenderloins into ¼-inch diagonal slices on cutting board—it's hard to do. Serve the tenderloins with remaining sauce.

Shape the meat mixture into a round mound with a 1-inch-deep "crater" in the center.

Prepare the Cheese Topping and pour it into the crater (or fill it with hot dog relish instead).

Crater Ham Loaf

6 servings.

Utensils	Ingredients
Medium bowl	2 eggs
Fork	1 pound ground fully
Square baking pan,	cooked smoked ham
9 × 9 × 2 inches	1 pound ground lean
	pork
	3 cups whole wheat
	flake cereal
	1 cup milk
	1 teaspoon salt
	⅛ teaspoon pepper
	Cheese Topping (right)

1   Heat oven to 375°.

2   Mix thoroughly all ingredients except Cheese Topping in bowl with fork until there are no streaks.

3   Place the meat mixture in ungreased baking pan. Shape with your hands into a round mound. Gently press down the center and build up the side to make a wall 1 inch high and 1 inch wide around the outside of the circle. There will be a 1-inch-deep "crater" in the center.

4   Prepare the Cheese Topping and pour it into the crater. Bake uncovered in 375° oven 1 hour or until golden brown on top.

Cheese Topping

Utensils	Ingredients
Small bowl	1 egg
Fork	2 tablespoons milk
	1 package (4 ounces)
	your favorite shredded
	cheese (about 1 cup)
	¼ teaspoon dry mustard
	¼ teaspoon Worcester-
	shire sauce

Beat 1 egg and 2 tablespoons milk in bowl with fork until blended. Stir in remaining ingredients. Now continue with Step 4.

Note: In place of the Cheese Topping, you can use 1 cup hot dog relish.

Baked Fish with Onion Rings

6 servings.

Utensils	Ingredients
Cutting board	2 packages (1 pound each) frozen skinless haddock fillets
Sharp knife	½ teaspoon salt
Oblong baking pan, 13 × 9 × 2 inches	2 tablespoons bottled lemon juice
Pancake turner	1 can (11 ounces) condensed Cheddar cheese soup
Fork	½ teaspoon paprika
	1 package (9 ounces) frozen French fried onions
	3 dill pickles

1 Heat oven to 475°.

2 Let the frozen fillets stand at room temperature 10 minutes for easier cutting.

3 Cut the fillets into 6 blocks of equal size on cutting board.

4 Place the blocks in ungreased baking pan. Sprinkle the blocks with ½ teaspoon salt and drizzle with 2 tablespoons lemon juice, making sure to get a little of each on each block of fish.

5 Turn the blocks over with pancake turner so salted sides are down. Separate each block from the others.

6 Stir the soup in the can with fork and pour it evenly over the blocks. Sprinkle with ½ teaspoon paprika. Cover with the frozen onions.

7 Bake uncovered in 475° oven 25 to 30 minutes or until the fish flakes easily with the fork and the onions are crisp.

8 While the fish is baking, cut each pickle crosswise into 5 or 6 slices.

9 Arrange 2 or 3 pickle slices on each serving.

Note: In place of the Cheddar cheese soup, you can use 1 can (10¾ ounces) condensed cream of shrimp soup. Omit the pickles.

Cook's Corner

Here are a few fishy facts:

Is fish really "brain food"? No. Eating fish won't make you any smarter, but you're smart if you eat fish. It's full of valuable protein and minerals to help you grow and stay healthy.

What are fish fillets? They're the sides of the fish, cut away from the backbone. Fillets are practically boneless.

What are fish sticks? They're "sticks" of fish that have been cut from frozen blocks of fish fillets. They're coated with batter, dipped in a crumb mixture, partly cooked, then frozen. You finish the cooking and serve them with fondue or in taco shells or other ways.

Do fish need lots of cooking? No! They're very tender to start with.

Crispy Fried Fish

3 or 4 servings.

Utensils	Ingredients
Small bowl	1 cup milk
Spoon	2 teaspoons salt
Pie pan	1 cup white cornmeal
Large skillet	¼ cup salad oil
Tongs	1 pound fish fillets*

1 Mix 1 cup milk and 2 teaspoons salt in small bowl. Empty 1 cup cornmeal into pie pan.

2 Heat ¼ cup oil in skillet over medium heat.

3 Dip each fillet in the milk, then in the cornmeal with tongs.

4 Place the coated fillets in the hot skillet and fry about 5 minutes on each side. (Do not overcook.) Drain.

*Haddock, pike, trout, perch, sunfish or crappies are all good fish to use.

Note: In place of the cornmeal, you can use 1 cup buttermilk baking mix.

This is a good way to cook freshly caught fish at home or over a campfire.

Fish Stick Fondue

6 servings.

Utensils	Ingredients
Cutting board	2 packages (7 or 8 ounces each) frozen breaded fish sticks
Sharp knife	
Cookie sheet or jelly roll pan, 15½ × 10½ × 1 inch	1 large dill pickle
2 small serving bowls	½ cup mayonnaise or salad dressing
Fork	½ teaspoon onion powder
Pancake turner	½ cup chili sauce
Serving platter	1 teaspoon horseradish
Fondue forks or wooden picks	1 teaspoon bottled lemon juice
	¼ teaspoon Worcestershire sauce
	Dash of salt

1 Heat oven to temperature given on fish stick package. Let the frozen fish sticks stand at room temperature 10 minutes for easier cutting.

2 Cut each fish stick crosswise into 3 equal pieces on cutting board. Place the fish stick pieces on ungreased cookie sheet.

3 Chop 1 pickle into ¼-inch pieces. Mix the chopped pickle, ½ cup mayonnaise and ½ teaspoon onion powder in serving bowl with fork.

4 Mix ½ cup chili sauce, 1 teaspoon horseradish, 1 teaspoon lemon juice, ¼ teaspoon Worcestershire sauce and dash of salt in another serving bowl with fork.

5 Bake the fish stick pieces as directed on package. Lift to platter with pancake turner. Serve the fish stick pieces with the 2 bowls of dips, along with fondue forks.

Tuna Casserole

6 servings.

Utensils	Ingredients
2-quart casserole with cover	1 package (about 7 ounces) macaroni shells
Large saucepan	3 tablespoons instant minced onion or ½ cup frozen chopped onion
Colander	1 celery stalk
Cutting board	1 package (8 ounces) pasteurized process cheese spread (loaf shape)
Sharp knife	2 cans (6½ ounces each) tuna
Fork	1 can (10¾ ounces) condensed cream of chicken soup
Long-handled spoon	Milk
	1 jar (2 ounces) sliced pimiento
	1 teaspoon bottled lemon juice

1 Heat oven to 375°. Grease casserole with shortening.

2 Cook the macaroni shells as directed on package.* Ask someone older to drain the shells for you. Pour them into the greased casserole. Sprinkle with 3 tablespoons minced onion.

3 Wash 1 celery stalk and pinch off leaves. Chop the celery into ½-inch pieces on cutting board. (If you like more crunch, cut up another celery stalk.) Add the cut-up celery to the macaroni shells and onion.

4 Cut about four ½-inch slices from the cheese loaf. Cut each slice into ½-inch squares until you have enough to measure 1 cup. Empty into the casserole. (Don't put the cheese away—you'll need it later.)

5 Empty the tuna into the colander to drain. Break the tuna into chunks with fork. Add to the casserole and stir. Pour the soup into the casserole. Fill the soup can half full with milk and stir with fork to get all the soup out. Pour the milk into the casserole.

6 Drain the jar of pimiento. Empty the pimiento into the casserole. Sprinkle with 1 teaspoon lemon juice and stir lightly until all ingredients are mixed.

7 Slice thin slices from remaining cheese loaf (enough to cover the top of the casserole). Place the slices on top of the casserole. Cover the casserole.

8 Bake in 375° oven 30 minutes. Uncover and bake 5 minutes.

* Or here's an easy way to cook the macaroni: Drop it into 6 cups rapidly boiling salted water (4 teaspoons salt). Heat until it boils rapidly again. Cook, stirring constantly, 3 minutes. Cover tightly, remove from the heat and let stand 10 minutes. Drain.

Note: In place of the cream of chicken soup, you can use 1 can (10¾ ounces) condensed cream of shrimp soup.

Pictured: Watermelon Star Salad (page 44)

SUPER SALADS AND VEGETABLES

Friendly Dog Salad

1 salad.

Utensils	Ingredients
Salad plate	1 lettuce leaf
Fork	1 canned pear half
Kitchen scissors	1 canned prune
Teaspoon	2 canned mandarin orange segments
	1 maraschino cherry
	1 raisin

1 Wash 1 lettuce leaf and pat dry with towel. Place on salad plate. Lift 1 pear half, 1 prune and 2 mandarin orange segments from cans and 1 maraschino cherry from jar with fork and drain. (Refrigerate remaining fruit with syrup for another time.)

2 Place the pear half cut side down on the lettuce leaf. Cut the prune lengthwise in half with scissors and take out pit. Place one of the prune halves at the large end of the pear half for the ear. (Eat the other prune half!)

3 Scoop out a tiny hole in the pear half for the eye with teaspoon. Place 1 raisin in the hole. Cut the maraschino cherry in half with the scissors. Place one half at the top of the narrow end of the pear half for the nose. (Eat the other cherry half!) Use the mandarin orange segments for the collar.

Fruits on Skewers

1 Place a pineapple chunk, a mandarin orange segment, a watermelon pickle and a maraschino cherry or a grape on a skewer. If there is room, repeat the fruits. Leave a little space on each end of the skewer. Repeat until you've filled as many skewers as you want with fruit.

2 Cut a thin slice from the stem end of an orange (so it won't roll around) and place the orange cut side down on a small plate. Poke the skewers into the orange. To eat the fruit, push it off the skewer with a fork.

Yellow-Haired Girl Salad

1 salad.

Utensils	Ingredients
Fork	1 ruffly lettuce leaf
Cutting board	1 canned peach half
Sharp knife	1 maraschino cherry
Salad plate	1 celery stalk
Kitchen scissors	1 large marshmallow
	10 raisins
	Shredded yellow cheese

1 Wash 1 lettuce leaf and pat dry with towel. Lift 1 peach half from can and 1 maraschino cherry from jar with fork and drain. (Refrigerate remaining peaches and cherries with syrup for another time.)

2 Wash 1 celery stalk and pinch off leaves. Cut the celery into thin strips about 2 inches long and ¼ inch wide on cutting

board. Keep 4 strips for your salad. (Refrigerate the rest for nibbles.)

3 Place the peach half cut side down in center of salad plate. Place 1 marshmallow at one end of the peach half for the head.

4 Place the celery strips at the sides and bottom of the peach half for arms and legs. Place 1 raisin at the end of each strip for hands and feet. Use raisins for eyes, nose and buttons too.

5 Place some shredded cheese around the marshmallow for hair. Cut a piece off the maraschino cherry with scissors to make mouth and place on marshmallow. (Eat the rest of the cherry!)

6 Now all your salad girl needs is a skirt, so tear a ruffly edge off the lettuce leaf and dress her with it. (Eat the rest of the lettuce or save it for the hamsters.)

Ham Roll-Ups with Cantaloupe Wedges

4 servings.

Utensils	Ingredients
Wooden picks	4 thin slices fully
Sharp knife	cooked smoked ham
Spoon	or 4 slices bologna
	1 small cantaloupe

1 Roll up each slice of ham as tightly as you can. Fasten with wooden picks.

2 Cut the cantaloupe into 4 wedges. Scoop out the seeds. Serve a ham roll with each melon wedge.

Firecracker Salads

6 salads.

Utensils	Ingredients
Cutting board	1 package (10 ounces) frozen sliced strawberries
Sharp knife	
Small saucepan	
2 small bowls	1 celery stalk
Long-handled spoon	1 cup water
Fork	1 package (3 ounces) strawberry-flavored gelatin
6 glasses (about 6 ounces each)	
Rubber scraper	½ cup frozen whipped topping, thawed
Tablespoon	½ cup miniature marshmallows
	½ cup blueberries

1 Remove the strawberries from freezer. Let stand at room temperature about 10 minutes so they thaw slightly.

2 Wash 1 celery stalk and pinch off leaves. Cut the celery into thin strips about 2 inches long and ¼ inch wide on cutting board. Keep 6 strips for your salads. (Refrigerate the rest for nibbles.)

3 Heat 1 cup water just to boiling in saucepan over medium-high heat. Empty the gelatin into bowl. Pour the boiling water over the gelatin. Stir until the gelatin dissolves. Stir in the slightly thawed strawberries. Break apart the clumps of strawberries with fork.

4 Pour the gelatin-strawberry mixture into 6 glasses, filling each glass about ⅓ of the way to the top. Refrigerate at least 2 hours or until the gelatin is firm.

5 Just before serving, empty ½ cup whipped topping into another bowl. Fold in ½ cup miniature marshmallows. Spoon about

2 tablespoons of the topping mixture onto the gelatin in each glass. Top with about 1 tablespoon blueberries. Poke 1 celery strip into the top of each salad to make the firecracker's fuse.

Watermelon Star Salad

Pictured on page 41.

1 salad.

Utensils	Ingredients
Salad plate	Lettuce leaf
Cutting board	½ slice medium watermelon (1 inch thick)
Sharp knife	
Tablespoon	½ cup creamed cottage cheese
	1 tablespoon blueberries

1 Wash 1 lettuce leaf and pat dry with towel. Place on salad plate.

2 Cut the watermelon slice into 5 wedges on cutting board. Cut the red melon away from the white part and green rind.

3 Arrange the melon wedges on the lettuce leaf in a circle with the points outward to make a star. Spoon ½ cup cottage cheese into the center of the watermelon star.

4 Sprinkle the cottage cheese with 1 tablespoon blueberries.

Porcupine Salads

6 salads.

Utensils	Ingredients
6 salad plates	6 lettuce leaves
Fork	6 canned peach halves
Kitchen scissors	12 maraschino cherries
Small bowl	1 package (3 ounces)
Teaspoon	cream cheese, softened*
	12 grapes
	Slivered almonds

1 Wash 6 lettuce leaves and pat dry with towel. Place 1 lettuce leaf on each salad plate. Lift 6 peach halves from can with fork and pat dry. (Refrigerate remaining peaches with syrup for another time.)

2 Cut 12 maraschino cherries into small pieces with scissors and empty into bowl. Stir in the cream cheese with fork and mix until blended. Drop a teaspoonful of the mixture onto the center of each lettuce leaf. Place a peach half cut side down to cover the mixture on each lettuce leaf.

3 Cut 6 grapes into 4 pieces each with the scissors. Place 4 pieces around each peach half for feet. Use 1 uncut grape for the head of each porcupine. Poke a few slivered almonds into the top of each peach half to look like porcupine quills.

*You can soften cream cheese the way you do butter—let it stand at room temperature for about an hour.

Note: You can change the porcupine salad to look like a prehistoric stegosaurus. Put the slivered almonds in a single row on the peach to look like rows of bony plates along a stegosaurus's spine.

Crunchy Coleslaw

4 or 5 servings.

Utensils	Ingredients
Cutting board	1 small head cabbage
Sharp knife	1 medium red apple
Medium bowl	1 cup miniature marsh-mallows
Apple corer	1 teaspoon bottled lemon juice
Fork	½ cup pineapple, lemon or lime yogurt
	2 tablespoons chopped nuts

1 Chop the cabbage into long shreds on cutting board, then chop the shreds into small pieces until you have enough to measure 2 cups. Place in bowl. (Wrap remaining cabbage and refrigerate to use another time.)

2 Wash and core 1 apple. Cut into quarters. Chop each quarter into ¼-inch pieces. Place in the bowl. Add 1 cup miniature marshmallows, 1 teaspoon lemon juice and ½ cup yogurt and toss with fork.

3 Sprinkle with 2 tablespoons chopped nuts.

Note: To shred cabbage in the blender, cut half the cabbage into 2-inch pieces and place in the blender container. Add cold water just to cover the cabbage. Cover the blender and follow the manufacturer's instructions or run just long enough to chop the cabbage, 3 to 4 seconds. Drain thoroughly and measure. Repeat with remaining cabbage if necessary to make 2 cups.

Start Your Own Kitchen Garden

Fold a piece of terry toweling into quarters and place it in the bottom of a loaf pan.

Saturate the towel with water, then sprinkle it evenly with a single layer of mustard seeds.

Place the loaf pan in a sunny window, and in 10 to 12 days the tiny plants will be ready to be harvested.

You can grow little plants from the mustard seeds in the kitchen spice cabinet to sprinkle over tossed salads and egg salad, meat and fish sandwich fillings. Try nibbling them all by themselves too—they're good!

1 Fold a piece of terry toweling (about 16 inches long and 8 inches wide) into quarters (about 8 inches long and 4 inches wide). Pat it evenly to cover the bottom of a loaf pan.

2 Pour water over the towel until it's saturated, then sprinkle mustard seeds on top in a single layer.

3 Cover with aluminum foil and leave overnight.

4 Remove the foil and place your planter in a warm, sunny place. Make sure that the towel always stays wet but not covered with water. The seeds will sprout and send roots into the towel. The plants will grow about an inch high, with tiny round green leaves, purple on the undersides, and long, thin stems.

5 Harvest the crop 10 to 12 days after you plant it, snipping the plants off at the base with scissors. (Garden cress, available from seed catalogs, can be grown this way too.)

Salad in a Bag

About 6 servings.

Utensils	Ingredients
Cutting board	1 medium head lettuce
Sharp knife	2 medium tomatoes
Plastic bag (about	8 radishes
12 inches long) with	⅓ cup your favorite
fastener	salad dressing
Large salad bowl	About 6 tablespoons
	shredded Cheddar
	cheese

1 Cut core from the lettuce on cutting board. Rinse the lettuce under running cold water. Throw away any bruised leaves. Tear remaining lettuce into bite-size chunks; drain.

2 Wash and cut stem ends from 2 tomatoes. Cut each tomato into 8 wedges. Wash and trim 8 radishes, then cut into thin slices.

3 Place the lettuce chunks, tomato wedges and radish slices in plastic bag. Pour in ⅓ cup salad dressing. (Someone should hold the bag while you pour or pour while you hold the bag.)

4 Close the bag tightly with fastener or hold it closed tightly. Then shake vigorously once or twice. Empty into salad bowl. Sprinkle with about 6 tablespoons shredded cheese.

Garlic Croutons

About 2 cups croutons.

Utensils	Ingredients
Cutting board	4 slices white bread
Sharp knife	Soft butter or margarine
Table knife	¼ teaspoon garlic
Cookie sheet	powder
Long-handled spoon	

1 Heat oven to 400°.

2 Trim crust from 4 slices bread on cutting board.

3 Spread both sides of the bread generously with soft butter. Sprinkle with ¼ teaspoon garlic powder. Cut into ½-inch squares and place on ungreased cookie sheet.

4 Bake in 400° oven 10 to 15 minutes or until golden brown and crisp, stirring occasionally.

5 Cool these crispy bread cubes, store them in a tightly covered container and add them to tossed green salads as you need them. Nice sprinkled over steaming hot soup too.

Cook's Corner

Do you eat 4 servings of fruits and vegetables each and every day? Be sure to include a citrus fruit or its juice (like orange and grapefruit), a deep yellow fruit or vegetable (like apricots and cantaloupe, carrots and winter squash), a dark green vegetable (like beans and broccoli) and something green and leafy (like cabbage and Brussels sprouts). These foods are chock full of important vitamins that help keep your skin healthy and help you to see in the dark.

Vegetable-Beef Soup

8 servings.

Utensils	Ingredients
Cutting board	3 celery stalks
Sharp knife	1 pound beef cubed
Dutch oven with cover	steaks
Pancake turner or	1 tablespoon shortening
tongs	1 package (10 ounces)
Long-handled spoon	frozen whole kernel
	corn
	1 package (9 ounces)
	frozen cut green
	beans
	1 package (9 ounces)
	frozen wax beans
	2 cups frozen sliced
	carrots (about 8
	ounces)
	1 envelope (about 1¼
	ounces) onion soup
	mix
	1 can (8 ounces) stewed
	tomatoes
	4 cups water
	2 teaspoons salt

1 Wash 3 celery stalks and pinch off leaves. Chop the celery into ½-inch pieces on cutting board.

2 Cut the cubed steaks into 1-inch pieces. Melt 1 tablespoon shortening in Dutch oven over medium-high heat. Add the steak pieces and cook, turning with pancake turner, until brown on both sides.

3 Stir in the chopped celery, corn, green beans, wax beans, 2 cups sliced carrots, the onion soup mix, stewed tomatoes (with liquid), 4 cups water and 2 teaspoons salt. Heat to boiling over medium-high heat, stirring constantly. Reduce heat. Cover and simmer over low heat 10 minutes.

Mashed Potatoes

4 to 6 servings.

Utensils	Ingredients
Vegetable parer	6 medium potatoes
Cutting board	Salt
Sharp knife	½ cup milk
Large saucepan with	3 tablespoons butter or
cover	margarine
Fork	¼ teaspoon salt
Colander	Parsley sprigs (if you
Potato masher	like)
Long-handled spoon	
Serving dish	
Scissors	

1 Wash and pare 6 potatoes. Cut each potato in half on cutting board.

2 Using a measuring cup, pour 1 inch of water into saucepan. Keep track of how many cups of water you use, then add ½ teaspoon salt for each cup of water. Add the potatoes. (The water should just cover them.)

3 Cover and cook over medium heat 20 to 25 minutes or until the potatoes are tender when pierced with fork. Ask someone older to drain the potatoes in colander.

4 Return the potatoes to the saucepan and mash with potato masher until no lumps remain. Add ½ cup milk, 3 tablespoons butter and ¼ teaspoon salt. Beat vigorously until light and fluffy.

5 Spoon the potatoes into serving dish. Snip some parsley onto the potatoes with scissors.

Crunchy Green Beans

4 servings.

Utensils	Ingredients
Spoon	1 can (16 ounces) French-style green beans
1-quart casserole with cover	1 can (10¾ ounces) condensed cream of mushroom soup
	1 can (3½ ounces) French-fried onions

1 Heat oven to 350°.

2 Drain the can of green beans.

3 Mix the green beans and half of the can of soup in ungreased casserole. Cover.

4 Bake in 350° oven 20 minutes.

5 Remove from oven. Arrange half of the can of onions on top. Bake uncovered 15 minutes.

Note: Cover and refrigerate remaining soup to use the next day. Fill the soup can half full with water and heat as directed. Just before serving, sprinkle remaining onions on top of the soup.

Buttered Carrot Sticks

4 servings.

Utensils	Ingredients
Vegetable parer	8 medium carrots
Cutting board	Salt
Sharp knife	2 tablespoons butter or margarine
Large saucepan with cover	
Fork	
Slotted spoon	
Serving dish	

1 Wash and pare 8 carrots, then cut lengthwise into ½-inch strips on cutting board.

2 Using a measuring cup, pour 1 inch of water into saucepan. Keep track of how many cups of water you use, then add ½ teaspoon salt for each cup of water. Add the carrots. (The water should just cover them.)

3 Cover and cook over medium heat 18 to 20 minutes or until the carrots are tender when pierced with fork.

4 Lift the carrots to serving dish with slotted spoon. Gently stir in 2 tablespoons butter.

Corn on the Cob

Utensils	Ingredients
Large kettle	Ears of sweet corn
Tongs	Sugar
Serving dish	Bottled lemon juice

1 Husk the ears of corn and remove silk just before cooking.

2 Place the ears in kettle. Using a measuring cup, pour in enough cold water to cover the ears. Keep track of how many cups of water you use, then add 1 tablespoon sugar and 1 tablespoon lemon juice for each gallon (16 cups) of water.

3 Heat to boiling over medium-high heat. Boil uncovered 2 minutes. Lift the corn to serving dish with tongs.

Cheese-Scalloped Corn

4 servings.

Utensils	Ingredients
1-quart casserole	1 can (17 ounces) cream-style corn
Spoon	2 eggs
Table knife	½ cup shredded Cheddar cheese
	½ teaspoon salt
	¼ cup dry bread crumbs

1 Heat oven to 350°.

2 Mix the corn, 2 eggs, ½ cup shredded cheese and ½ teaspoon salt in ungreased casserole. Sprinkle with ¼ cup bread crumbs. Bake the corn uncovered in 350° oven 35 minutes.

Easy Baked Squash

4 to 6 servings.

Utensils	Ingredients
1½-quart casserole with cover	2 packages (12 ounces each) frozen squash
Table knife	2 tablespoons butter or margarine
Spoon	½ teaspoon salt
	2 tablespoons instant minced onion

1 Heat oven to 425°.

2 Empty the frozen squash into ungreased casserole. Cut 2 tablespoons butter into pieces and dot the top of the squash with the pieces. Sprinkle with ½ teaspoon salt. Cover.

3 Bake in 425° oven 30 minutes.

4 Remove from oven and stir in 2 tablespoons minced onion. Cover and bake 10 minutes.

Pictured: Frozen Dough Fun (page 65)

A BUNCH OF BREADS

Chunky Tuna Sandwiches

6 sandwiches.

Utensils	Ingredients
Medium bowl	1 can (6½ ounces) tuna
Cutting board	1 celery stalk
Sharp knife	1 large kosher dill pickle
Fork	¼ cup mayonnaise or salad dressing
Table knife or spatula	¼ teaspoon onion salt
	¼ teaspoon bottled lemon juice
	12 slices white or whole wheat bread
	Soft butter or margarine

1 Drain the can of tuna, then place the tuna in bowl.

2 Wash 1 celery stalk and pinch off leaves. Chop the celery and 1 pickle into ¼-inch pieces on cutting board. Place in the bowl with the tuna.

3 Stir in ¼ cup mayonnaise, ¼ teaspoon onion salt and ¼ teaspoon lemon juice with fork.

4 Spread 12 slices bread with soft butter, then spread half of them with the tuna mixture and cover with remaining slices to make 6 sandwiches. Refrigerate any leftovers.

VARIATION

Hot Tuna Sandwiches: Follow recipe for Chunky Tuna Sandwiches except—heat oven to 375°. In place of the bread, use 3 hamburger buns, cut in half. Place the halves on an ungreased cookie sheet. Omit the butter. Spread each bun half with about 1/6 of the tuna mixture. Wash and cut stem end from 1 medium tomato. Cut it into 6 slices on the cutting board. Place 1 slice on each bun half and sprinkle with a little salt. Cover each tomato slice with 1 slice process American cheese and sprinkle with a little paprika. Bake in 375° oven 8 minutes or until the cheese melts.

Cook's Corner

Hard-cooked eggs are very easy to make, and there are lots of things you can do with them: You need them for the Egg Salad-Peanut Sandwiches on the facing page. A hard-cooked egg and a tiny saltshaker packed in a pocket when you go out for a hike makes a terrific snack. Or pop one into your lunch box for some extra protein power. You can refrigerate hard-cooked eggs for up to 7 days, so make a few to have around for when you want them.

To prepare hard-cooked eggs, place as many eggs as you want to cook in a saucepan with a cover. Add enough cold water to come at least 1 inch above the eggs. Heat to boiling over medium-high heat. Remove from the heat and cover. Let stand 22 to 24 minutes.

Uncover the saucepan and place it in the sink. Run cold water into the pan to cool the eggs quickly. (This makes the eggs easier to shell and keeps the yolks from turning dark around the edges.)

To shell the eggs, tap each one on the kitchen counter to crack the shell. Roll it between your hands to loosen the shell. Hold it under cold water as you peel it.

Egg Salad-Peanut Sandwiches

4 sandwiches.

Utensils	Ingredients
Cutting board	3 hard-cooked eggs*
Sharp knife	1 celery stalk
Medium bowl	¼ cup salted peanuts
Spoon	3 tablespoons mayon-
Table knife	naise or salad
	dressing
	¼ teaspoon onion salt
	⅛ teaspoon salt
	Soft butter or margarine
	8 slices rye or whole
	wheat bread

1 Peel 3 hard-cooked eggs.

2 Wash 1 celery stalk and pinch off leaves. (Keep them to feed the gerbils or add to a salad for decoration.)

3 Chop the celery and ¼ cup peanuts into very small pieces and the eggs into ¼-inch pieces on cutting board. Place in bowl.

4 Stir in 3 tablespoons mayonnaise, ¼ teaspoon onion salt and ⅛ teaspoon salt.

5 Spread 8 slices bread with soft butter, then spread half of them with the egg mixture and cover with remaining slices to make 4 sandwiches. Cut each sandwich in half and serve right away. Refrigerate any leftover sandwiches.

* To hard-cook eggs, see the facing page.

VARIATION

Egg Salad Sandwiches: Follow recipe for Egg Salad-Peanut Sandwiches except—omit the peanuts.

Baked Cheese Sandwich

1 sandwich.

Utensils	Ingredients
Table knife	1 or 2 slices process
Cookie sheet	American cheese
	2 slices white or dark
	rye bread
	Soft butter or margarine

1 Heat oven to 450°.

2 Place 1 or 2 slices cheese between 2 slices bread. Spread outsides of the sandwich with soft butter. Place on ungreased cookie sheet.

3 Bake in 450° oven about 12 minutes or until the cheese melts and the bread is golden brown.

Note: Instead of baking the sandwich, you can cook it in a skillet over low heat until golden brown, about 5 minutes. (Lift an edge and peek.) Turn with a pancake turner and cook about 5 minutes on the other side or until the cheese melts. Watch carefully so it doesn't burn.

Or if you have a microwave oven, you can cook the sandwich in that. Do not butter the outsides of the sandwich. Wrap it in a paper napkin and place it on a paper plate. Cook in the microwave oven about 45 seconds or until the sandwich is hot. Remove it from the oven, unwrap it and spread the outsides with soft butter or margarine.

Beat the dough vigorously with a fork until it cleans the side of the bowl.

To knead, curve your fingers and fold the dough toward you, then push it away with the heels of your hands.

Roll each part of dough into an oval on an ungreased cookie sheet, then pinch up a rim around the edge.

Top the dough with some of the tomato sauce mixture, shredded cheese and frankfurter slices.

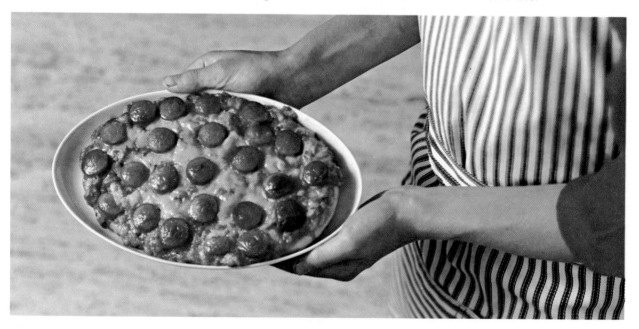

Polka Dot Pizzas

3 pizzas.

Utensils	Ingredients
Breadboard	2 cans (8 ounces each) tomato sauce
Medium bowl	3 tablespoons instant minced onion or ½ cup frozen chopped onion
2 forks	
Large bowl	
Cookie sheet	2 teaspoons oregano leaves
Rolling pin	
Rubber scraper	¼ teaspoon pepper
Cutting board	2½ cups buttermilk baking mix
Sharp knife	1 package active dry yeast
	⅔ cup hot water
	2 cups shredded Cheddar or mozzarella cheese (about 8 ounces)
	6 skinless frankfurters

1 Heat oven to 425°. Rub some flour into breadboard to cover about a 10-inch area.

2 Mix the tomato sauce, 3 tablespoons minced onion, 2 teaspoons oregano and ¼ teaspoon pepper in medium bowl with fork. (You'll use this later for a topping.)

3 Mix 2½ cups baking mix and the yeast in large bowl with another fork. Stir in ⅔ cup hot water and beat vigorously until the dough cleans the side of the bowl.

4 Gently smooth the dough into a ball on the floured board. Knead 20 times. Allow the dough to rest a few minutes, then divide the dough into 3 equal parts.

5 Shape 1 part into a ball and place it in the center of ungreased cookie sheet. Rub a little flour on rolling pin and roll the ball into an oval ¼ inch thick. Pinch the edge to make a little stand-up rim.

6 Dip out ⅓ of the tomato sauce mixture (about ⅔ cup) and pour onto the oval. Spread the sauce mixture almost to the edge of the dough with rubber scraper. Sprinkle with ⅓ of the shredded cheese (about ⅔ cup).

7 Cut 2 of the frankfurters crosswise into penny slices on cutting board. Arrange the slices on the pizza.

8 Bake in 425° oven 15 to 20 minutes or until the crust is golden brown.

9 Repeat steps 5 through 8 with 2 remaining parts of dough and remaining sauce, cheese and frankfurters to make 2 more pizzas.

Note: You may want to gobble up the pizzas as they come out of the oven. If not, this is a good bake-ahead recipe. When you're ready to eat, heat the pizzas, 2 at a time, on an ungreased cookie sheet in a 300° oven about 5 minutes or until hot. The third pizza will be ready by the time you've finished eating the first 2.

Be sure to eat 4 servings of enriched or whole-grain breads and cereals every day. (You can have 1 cup cold cereal or ½ cup cooked cereal or ½ to ¾ cup cooked macaroni or rice instead of 1 slice of bread.) These foods give you quick energy and help your body do its work.

Toasty Hot Dog Roll-Ups

8 roll-ups.

Utensils	Ingredients
Medium saucepan with cover	2 cups water
Small saucepan	8 frankfurters
Cookie sheet	½ cup butter or mar- garine (1 stick)
Pastry brush	8 slices white bread
Table knife	2 teaspoons prepared mustard
Tongs or fork	4 slices process American cheese
16 wooden picks	Catsup

1 Heat oven to 375°.

2 Heat 2 cups water to boiling in medium saucepan over medium heat. Carefully drop 8 frankfurters into the water. Reduce heat. Cover and simmer over low heat 5 to 8 minutes.

3 Melt ½ cup butter in small saucepan over low heat.

4 Place 8 slices bread on ungreased cookie sheet. Brush the top sides of the slices with about half of the melted butter. Spread with 2 teaspoons mustard (about ¼ teaspoon for each slice).

5 Cut 4 slices cheese diagonally in half so you have 8 cheese triangles. Top each bread slice with 1 cheese triangle.

6 Place 1 frankfurter on top of each cheese triangle with tongs.

7 Fold the bread over to make a triangle shape. Fasten with 2 wooden picks, 1 on each side, poking them through the bread and frankfurter. Brush the outside of the bread triangles with remaining melted butter.

8 Bake in 375° oven 10 to 15 minutes or until golden brown. Serve with catsup.

Note: In place of the mustard, you can spread the buttered bread with 2 teaspoons horseradish or pickle relish.

Open-Face Hamburgers

4 hamburgers.

Utensils	Ingredients
Medium bowl	½ slice white bread
Fork	½ pound ground beef
Toaster	¼ cup milk
Cookie sheet	½ teaspoon salt
Table knife	¼ teaspoon onion powder
	4 slices white bread

1 Heat oven to 400°.

2 Tear ½ slice bread into tiny pieces and place in bowl. Stir in the ground beef, ¼ cup milk, ½ teaspoon salt and ¼ tea- spoon onion powder with fork.

3 Toast 4 slices bread and place on un- greased cookie sheet.

4 Spread each slice of toast with about ¼ of the ground beef mixture. Cover the edges of the toast completely to prevent them from burning—no crusts should show.

5 Bake in 400° oven about 15 minutes. (If you're not sure if the hamburgers are done, ask for another opinion.)

French Toast

6 servings.

Utensils	Ingredients
Griddle	2 eggs
Small bowl	½ cup milk
Fork	¼ teaspoon salt
Pastry brush	6 slices day-old white or
Pancake turner	raisin bread
	Powdered sugar

1 Heat griddle over medium heat or heat electric griddle to 375°.

2 Beat 2 eggs, ½ cup milk and ¼ teaspoon salt in bowl with fork until blended.

3 Grease the hot griddle with a thin layer of butter or margarine, using pastry brush.

4 Dip 6 slices bread one at a time into the egg mixture.

5 Cook the bread on the greased hot griddle until golden brown, about 4 minutes. (Lift an edge and peek.) Turn with pancake turner and cook about 4 minutes on the other side. Serve with powdered sugar.

Remember this whenever you use the toaster: If the toast doesn't pop up by itself, pull out the plug and get some help from someone older. *Never try to pull out the toast with a fork or knife while the toaster is still connected—you could get a very nasty electric shock!*

Waffles

6 to 8 waffles.

Utensils	Ingredients
Waffle iron	2 eggs
Medium bowl	2 cups buttermilk
Egg beater	2 cups all-purpose flour*
Cup or pitcher	2 teaspoons baking
Fork	powder
	1 teaspoon baking soda
	½ teaspoon salt
	6 tablespoons shortening
	Butter or margarine
	Maple-flavored syrup

1 Heat waffle iron.

2 Beat 2 eggs in bowl until the whites and yellows are mixed. Add remaining ingredients except the butter and syrup and beat until smooth.

3 For each waffle, pour the batter from cup onto the center of the hot waffle iron. (Use about ⅔ cup batter in a 7-inch round waffle iron or about 1⅓ cups batter in a 9-inch square waffle iron.)

4 Cook about 5 minutes or until steaming stops. Remove the waffle carefully with fork. Serve with butter and syrup.

* If using self-rising flour, omit the baking powder and salt.

VARIATION

Blueberry Waffles: Follow recipe for waffles except—sprinkle 2 tablespoons blueberries over the batter for each waffle as soon as it's been poured onto the waffle iron.

Indian Maize Pancakes

Pictured on the facing page.

About 16 pancakes.

Utensils	Ingredients
Griddle	1 can (8 ounces) whole
Cup	kernel corn
Spoon	1 egg
Medium bowl	1¼ cups all-purpose
Egg beater	flour*
Pastry brush	2 tablespoons shortening
Pancake turner	1 teaspoon sugar
	1 teaspoon baking
	powder
	½ teaspoon baking soda
	½ teaspoon salt
	1¼ to 1½ cups butter-
	milk
	Homemade Pancake
	Syrup (right)

1 Heat griddle over medium heat or heat electric griddle to 375°.

2 Drain the liquid from the can of corn into cup. Spoon out ½ cup corn from the can and set aside. Pour the liquid in the cup back into the can and save the corn for another time.

3 Beat 1 egg in bowl until the white and yellow are mixed.

4 Add 1¼ cups flour, 2 tablespoons shortening, 1 teaspoon sugar, 1 teaspoon baking powder, ½ teaspoon baking soda and ½ teaspoon salt. Gradually add 1¼ to 1½ cups buttermilk.** Beat until smooth. Stir in the ½ cup corn.

5 Grease the hot griddle with shortening if necessary, using pastry brush. For each pancake, pour ¼ cup batter in a pool onto the hot griddle.

6 Cook until bubbles appear. Turn with pancake turner and cook until golden brown on the other side. (Lift an edge and peek.) Serve with Homemade Pancake Syrup.

* If using self-rising flour, omit the baking powder, baking soda and salt.

** If you like thick pancakes, use 1¼ cups; if you like thinner pancakes, use 1½ cups.

Homemade Pancake Syrup

1¾ cups syrup.

Utensils	Ingredients
Small saucepan	1½ cups brown sugar
Long-handled spoon	(packed)
	¾ cup water
	1 tablespoon butter or
	margarine
	Dash of salt
	½ teaspoon maple
	flavoring

1 Mix 1½ cups brown sugar, ¾ cup water, 1 tablespoon butter and dash of salt in saucepan.

2 Heat to boiling over medium heat, stirring constantly. Remove from heat. Stir in ½ teaspoon maple flavoring. Serve warm.

Apple-Sausage Pancakes

Pictured on page 58.

About 18 pancakes.

Utensils	Ingredients
Griddle	2 packages (8 ounces each) fully cooked brown and serve link sausages
Large skillet	
Small saucepan	
Pastry brush	
Medium bowl	1 can (21 ounces) apple pie filling
Egg beater	
Pancake turner	2 cups buttermilk baking mix
Table knife	
Serving plate	1 egg
Spoon	1⅓ to 1½ cups milk
	Butter or margarine

1 Heat griddle over medium heat or heat electric griddle to 375°.

2 Heat the sausages in skillet as directed on package. Heat the pie filling in saucepan over low heat. Keep the sausages and pie filling warm over very low heat while you prepare pancakes.

3 Grease the hot griddle with shortening if necessary, using pastry brush.

4 Prepare Pancakes as directed for thinner pancakes on baking mix package except—after mixing, for each pancake pour ¼ cup batter in an oval shape (about 5 inches long and 3 inches wide) onto the hot griddle. Continue as directed on the package.

5 Spread each pancake with butter and wrap it around a hot sausage. Place folded side down on plate and top with a spoonful of the hot pie filling.

Round-Up Pancakes

Pictured on page 58.

About 18 pancakes.

Utensils	Ingredients
Griddle	2 cups buttermilk baking mix
Pastry brush	
Medium bowl	1 egg
Egg beater	1⅓ cups milk
Teaspoon	Your favorite syrup
Pancake turner	

1 Heat griddle over medium heat or heat electric griddle to 375°. Grease the hot griddle with shortening if necessary, using pastry brush.

2 Prepare Pancakes as directed on baking mix package except—after mixing, drizzle some batter from teaspoon onto the hot griddle to form an initial. (Initials must be made backward to make them appear right when the pancakes are served.)

3 When the bottom side of the initial has browned, pour about ¼ cup batter over the initial.

4 Continue as directed on the package. Serve with syrup.

Surprise Muffins

18 muffins.

Utensils	Ingredients
2 or 3 muffin pans	1 egg
18 paper baking cups (if you like)	1 cup milk
	¼ cup salad oil
Medium bowl	2 cups all-purpose flour*
Fork	¼ cup sugar
Small bowl	3 teaspoons baking powder
Large spoon	
Teaspoon	1 teaspoon salt
Spatula	About 3 tablespoons jelly

1 Heat oven to 400°. Grease the bottoms of 18 muffin cups with shortening or line with baking cups.

2 Beat 1 egg, 1 cup milk and ¼ cup oil in medium bowl with fork until blended.

3 Mix 2 cups flour, ¼ cup sugar, 3 teaspoons baking powder and 1 teaspoon salt in small bowl. Add all at once to the egg mixture. Stir just until the flour is moistened—the batter will look lumpy.

4 Spoon the batter into the muffin cups, filling each cup ⅓ full. Drop ½ teaspoon jelly onto the center of each and top with enough batter to fill ⅔ full. Wipe off any batter spilled on the pans.

5 Bake in 400° oven 20 to 25 minutes or until golden brown. Loosen the muffins with spatula and remove them at once or tip them on their sides in the pans to prevent them from steaming and getting soggy.

* If using self-rising flour, omit the baking powder and salt.

Blueberry Coffee Cake

Utensils	Ingredients
Square baking pan, 9 x 9 x 2 inches	1 package (13.5 ounces) wild blueberry muffin mix
Medium bowl	1 egg
Fork	½ cup milk
Wooden pick	Streusel Topping (below)

1 Heat oven to 400°. Grease baking pan with shortening.

2 Prepare the muffin mix as directed on package except—after mixing, pour the batter into the greased pan. Sprinkle with Streusel Topping.

3 Bake in 400° oven 20 to 25 minutes or until wooden pick inserted in the center comes out clean. Serve warm.

Streusel Topping

Utensils	Ingredients
Small bowl	½ cup brown sugar (packed)
Fork	⅓ cup all-purpose flour
	¼ cup butter or margarine (½ stick)
	½ teaspoon cinnamon

Mix ½ cup brown sugar, ⅓ cup flour, ¼ cup butter and ½ teaspoon cinnamon in small bowl with fork until crumbly. Now continue with Step 2.

Cheesy Pretzels

16 pretzels.

Utensils	Ingredients
Cookie sheet	1½ cups all-purpose
Breadboard and	flour*
pastry cloth	⅔ cup milk
Rolling pin and	½ cup shredded Cheddar
stockinet cover	cheese (about 2
Custard cup	ounces)
Medium bowl	2 tablespoons butter or
Fork	margarine, softened
Table knife	2 teaspoons baking
Small bowl	powder
Pastry brush	1 teaspoon sugar
Pancake turner	1 teaspoon salt
Wire cooling rack	1 egg
	Coarse salt

1 Heat oven to 400°. Grease cookie sheet with shortening.

2 Cover breadboard with pastry cloth, tucking ends underneath. Cover rolling pin with stockinet cover. For convenience, place some flour in custard cup. Sprinkle the covered board and rolling pin lightly with the flour and rub it in until it disappears.

3 Mix 1½ cups flour, ⅔ cups milk, ½ cup shredded cheese, 2 tablespoons butter, 2 teaspoons baking powder, 1 teaspoon sugar, and 1 teaspoon salt to a soft dough in medium bowl with fork.

4 Gently smooth the dough into a ball on the covered board. Knead 10 times. Divide the dough in half.

5 Roll one half of the dough into a rectangle, 12 inches long and 8 inches wide. Mark and cut the rectangle lengthwise into eight 1-inch strips. Make each strip narrower by folding it lengthwise in half. Pinch the edges to seal.

6 Twist each strip into a pretzel shape and place seam side down on the greased cookie sheet.

7 Beat 1 egg in small bowl with the fork until the white and yellow are mixed.

8 Brush the pretzels with the beaten egg, then sprinkle lightly with coarse salt.

9 Bake in 400° oven 20 to 25 minutes or until golden brown. Lift with pancake turner to rack.

10 Repeat steps 5 through 10 with remaining half of the dough.

* If using self-rising flour, omit the baking powder and salt.

Note: In place of the coarse salt, you can use onion salt or garlic salt or grated American cheese food.

VARIATION

Peanutty Pretzels: Follow recipe for Cheesy Pretzels except—in place of the butter, use 2 tablespoons crunchy peanut butter. Omit the shredded cheese. In place of the coarse salt, use 2 tablespoons chopped salted peanuts.

A pastry cloth to cover your breadboard and a stockinet for your rolling pin are inexpensive and handy to have. The flour you rub into the cloth keeps dough or pastry from sticking when you roll it out. The extra flour doesn't get rolled into the dough or pastry either, so whatever you bake will be tender and delicious.

Roll half of the dough into a rectangle, 12 by 8 inches, then mark it and cut it into eight 1-inch strips.

Fold each strip lengthwise in half to make it narrower. Pinch the edges together tightly to seal it.

Twist each strip to make a pretzel shape, then put the pretzels seam sides down on a greased cookie sheet.

Brush the pretzels with beaten egg, then sprinkle them with a little coarse salt.

Butter Dips

18 dips.

Utensils	Ingredients
Breadboard and pastry cloth	¼ cup butter or margarine (½ stick)
Rolling pin and stockinet cover	1¼ cups all-purpose flour*
Custard cup	⅔ cup milk
Square baking pan, 9 × 9 × 2 inches	2 teaspoons sugar
Medium bowl	2 teaspoons baking powder
Fork	1 teaspoon salt
Sharp knife	

1 Heat oven to 450°. Cover breadboard with pastry cloth, tucking ends underneath. Cover rolling pin with stockinet cover. For convenience, place some flour in custard cup. Sprinkle the covered board and rolling pin lightly with the flour and rub it in until it disappears.

2 Melt ¼ cup butter in baking pan in oven. Mix 1¼ cups flour, ⅔ cup milk, 2 teaspoons sugar, 2 teaspoons baking powder and 1 teaspoon salt to a soft dough in bowl with fork.

3 Gently smooth the dough into a ball on the covered board. Knead 10 times. Roll the dough into an 8-inch square. Cut the square in half, then cut each half crosswise into 9 strips. (Dip the knife in flour to keep the dough from sticking.)

4 Dip each strip into the melted butter, turning to coat completely. Arrange the strips close together in 2 rows in the pan. Bake 15 to 20 minutes or until golden brown.

* If using self-rising flour, omit the baking powder and salt.

Birdseed Bread

Utensils	Ingredients
Medium bowl	2 cups buttermilk baking mix
Fork	½ cup cold water
Cookie sheet	¼ teaspoon garlic powder
Small saucepan	2 tablespoons butter or margarine
Pastry brush	2 tablespoons sesame seeds
Rubber scraper	2 tablespoons salted sunflower nuts or chopped nuts
Table knife	

1 Heat oven to 425°. Mix 2 cups baking mix, ½ cup cold water and ¼ teaspoon garlic powder to a soft dough in bowl with fork.

2 Pat the dough on ungreased cookie sheet into a 10-inch circle.

3 Melt 2 tablespoons butter in saucepan over low heat. Remove from heat. Brush the dough circle with the melted butter. Sprinkle with 2 tablespoons sesame seeds and 2 tablespoons sunflower nuts. Firmly press the seeds and nuts into the dough with rubber scraper.

4 Cut the circle into 12 equal wedges (like a pie).

5 Bake in 425° oven 15 to 20 minutes or until golden brown. Serve warm. (The bread will break into wedges.)

Frozen Dough Fun

Pictured on page 51.

1 large or 2 medium or 6 small figures.

Utensils	Ingredients
Cookie sheet	1 loaf (about 16 ounces)
Breadboard and pastry cloth	frozen bread dough
Rolling pin and stockinet cover	1 egg
3 custard cups	¼ cup milk or water
White paper	Honey Dip (right)
Pencil	
Kitchen scissors	
Fork	
Pancake turner	
Pastry brush	

1 Thaw the frozen dough (wrapped) in refrigerator overnight or at room temperature no longer than 6 hours. If more than 1 loaf comes in package, take out 1 loaf and wrap it loosely to thaw. Return remaining frozen dough in package to freezer.

2 When the dough has thawed, heat oven to 350°. Grease cookie sheet with shortening.

3 Cover breadboard with pastry cloth, tucking ends underneath. Cover rolling pin with stockinet cover. For convenience, place some flour in a custard cup. Sprinkle the covered board and rolling pin lightly with the flour and rub it in until it disappears.

4 Draw and cut out one or more patterns about 9 inches long and 7 inches wide.

5 Beat 1 egg with fork in another custard cup until the white and yellow are mixed. (You'll use this later for a glaze.) Pour ¼ cup milk into another custard cup. (You'll use this later for a kind of glue.)

6 Roll the thawed dough into a rectangle about 9 inches long, 7 inches wide and ¼ to ½ inch thick on the covered board.

7 Spread 1 or 2 drops of the milk on the back of the pattern, then place the pattern wet side down on top of the dough. Cut around the pattern with the scissors.

8 Lift the cut-out dough with pancake turner to the greased cookie sheet. Gently peel off the pattern. Pat down or reshape the dough as you like. Cut out pieces from the dough scraps to use for eyes, hair, feet or decorations. Dip the pieces in the milk to make them stick, then attach them.

9 Brush the dough figure with the beaten egg. Bake in 350° oven 25 minutes or until golden brown.

10 Is your dough figure too beautiful to eat? If you do decide to eat it, stir up some Honey Dip, break off chunks of bread and dip them in the dip.

Note: To make markings such as owl's feathers, make snips in the dough with scissors before baking. To add teeth to animals such as an alligator, stick miniature marshmallows to its open mouth with dabs of ready-to-spread frosting after the figure is baked and cooled.

Honey Dip

Utensils	Ingredients
Small bowl	¼ cup butter or
Fork	margarine, softened
	¼ cup honey
	Nutmeg

Beat ¼ cup butter and ¼ cup honey with fork in bowl. Sprinkle with a little nutmeg.

Wheaten Loaf

Utensils

Loaf pan,
   8½ × 4½ × 2½ or
   9 × 5 × 3 inches
Pastry brush
Large mixer bowl
Long-handled spoon
Electric mixer
Rubber scraper
Wire cooling rack

Ingredients

1 package active dry
   yeast
1¼ cups warm water
   (105 to 115°)
2 tablespoons honey,
   brown sugar or light
   molasses
2 tablespoons shortening
2 teaspoons salt
1 cup whole wheat flour
2 cups all-purpose flour*
Soft butter or margarine

1 Generously grease loaf pan with shortening, using pastry brush.

2 Dissolve the yeast in 1¼ cups warm water in mixer bowl. Stir in 2 tablespoons honey, 2 tablespoons shortening, 2 teaspoons salt, 1 cup whole wheat flour and ½ cup of the all-purpose flour. Beat on medium speed until smooth, about 2 minutes. Turn off the mixer occasionally and scrape the side of the bowl. Stir in remaining flour and mix until smooth, about 1½ minutes.

3 Cover and let rise in a warm place (85°) about 30 minutes or until an impression remains when the batter is touched lightly.

4 Stir down the batter by beating with the rubber scraper about 25 strokes.

5 Spread the batter in the greased pan. Rub some flour on your hands and pat the loaf gently to smooth the top. (The batter will be sticky.)

6 Let rise until the batter is ¼ inch from the top of the 8½-inch pan or 1 inch from the top of the 9-inch pan, about 40 minutes.

7 Ten minutes before baking the bread, heat oven to 375°.

8 Bake in 375° oven 45 to 50 minutes or until the loaf is brown and sounds hollow when tapped on top. Immediately remove the loaf from the pan and place on rack.

9 Brush the top of the loaf with soft butter. Cool thoroughly before slicing.

* If using self-rising flour, omit the salt.

Cook's Corner

To make a warming tent for the Wheaten Loaf yeast batter (or other bread dough) to rise in, fill a large bowl ⅔ full of hot water. Cover it with a wire cooling rack and place the bowl of batter on the rack. Completely cover the 2 bowls and the rack with a kitchen towel. Let the batter rise as directed in Step 3 of the recipe. After your unbaked loaf is in the pan, pour fresh hot water into the large bowl. Add the rack, the loaf pan and the towel and let rise as directed in Step 6.

Pictured: Peach Double Deckers (page 75)

DIFFERENT DESSERTS

Raspberry Ice Cream

4 quarts ice cream.

Utensils	Ingredients
Electric ice-cream freezer*	4 packages (10 ounces each) frozen raspberries
Dishpan or roasting pan	2 cups sugar
Blender	2 quarts (8 cups) half-and-half
Long-handled spoon	Ice cubes or crushed ice (about 6 quarts)
Large bowl	About 2 cups rock salt
Waxed paper (if you like)	

1 Thaw the frozen raspberries as directed on package.

2 Take ice-cream can (with dasher inside) out of ice-cream freezer and chill it in freezer or refrigerator.

3 Place the ice-cream freezer in dishpan to catch water that will drain from the hole in side of the freezer. Fit the chilled ice-cream can into the freezer. Fit the dasher into place in the can.

4 Empty 1 package thawed raspberries into blender container. Cover and blend on low speed 10 seconds or until the berries are liquid. Pour into the ice-cream can. Repeat, one package at a time, with remaining berries.

5 Empty 2 cups sugar into the ice-cream can. Pour in 2 quarts half-and-half and stir about 1 minute to dissolve the sugar.

6 Put the cover on the ice-cream can and fasten the top of the freezer with the help of someone older. Drop ice cubes (small ones work best) around the ice-cream can to a depth of about 3 inches. Sprinkle with ½ cup rock salt.

7 Plug in the freezer. (First be sure your hands are dry!) As the can turns, keep adding a 3-inch layer of ice and ½ cup rock salt around it until the top of the can is covered.

8 As the ice melts, keep adding ice and rock salt for 30 to 40 minutes or until the can starts to turn with difficulty.

9 Pull the plug and disconnect the motor. Lift the ice-cream can out of the freezer and pry off the cover (with the help of someone older). Lift the dasher into bowl. (Now's the time to lick the dasher!)

10 Serve the ice cream now if you like it soft and swirly. If you like firm ice cream, cover the can with waxed paper and freeze 4 hours.

* If you have a crank-type freezer, ask someone older to show you how to operate it. The results will be the same.

VARIATION

Raspberry Refrigerator Ice Cream: Follow recipe for Raspberry Ice Cream except—use only 1 package (10 ounces) frozen raspberries, ½ cup sugar and 1 pint (2 cups) half-and-half. After blending, pour into ice cube tray. Stir with a fork to break any bubbles. Freeze about 8 hours or until firm.

Caramel Applesauce

6 servings.

Utensils	Ingredients
Vegetable parer	6 medium apples
Apple corer	3 tablespoons butter or
Cutting board	margarine
Sharp knife	½ cup brown sugar
Medium saucepan with	(packed)
cover	½ cup water
Long-handled spoon	¼ teaspoon nutmeg
Fork	

1 Wash, pare and core 6 apples. Cut each apple into quarters on cutting board. Cut each quarter into 4 slices.

2 Heat 3 tablespoons butter and ½ cup brown sugar in saucepan over low heat until the butter melts.

3 Remove the saucepan from heat. Stir in the apple slices and mix gently until slices are coated with the butter and brown sugar.

4 Add ½ cup water and ¼ teaspoon nutmeg. (The apples will cook down and add more liquid.)

5 Return the saucepan to heat. Heat to boiling over medium-high heat, stirring occasionally. Reduce heat. Cover and simmer over low heat about 20 minutes or until apples are tender when pierced with fork. Stir once or twice. Serve warm or cold.

Cook's Corner

Superfruit! That's what these jiffy fruit desserts are—superquick to fix, supergood for you and super-delicious to eat!

• Canned fruit cocktail mixed with chopped unpared apple

• Orange slices sprinkled with flaked coconut

• Orange sections arranged like flower petals, with a cherry in the center

• Peach and pear halves with a spoonful of whipped topping, cranberry sauce or your favorite flavor jelly in the centers

• Banana slices mixed with strawberries

• Cantaloupe pieces mixed with grapes

Rhubarberry Sauce

6 servings.

Utensils	Ingredients
Medium saucepan	2 cups strawberries
Long-handled fork	½ cup water
	1 package (16 ounces)
	frozen rhubarb
	2 tablespoons sugar
	⅛ teaspoon ginger

1 Wash 2 cups strawberries and remove stems.

2 Heat ½ cup water to boiling in saucepan over medium-high heat. Add the rhubarb and 2 tablespoons sugar. Reduce heat. Simmer over low heat 5 minutes, stirring with fork to break the rhubarb apart. Remove from heat.

3 Stir in the strawberries and ⅛ teaspoon ginger. Serve warm or cold.

Marshmallow Custards

6 custards.

Utensils	Ingredients
Six 6-ounce custard cups	1½ cups miniature marshmallows
Oblong baking pan, 13 × 9 × 2 inches	3 eggs
Small bowl	⅓ cup sugar
Egg beater	Dash of salt
Medium saucepan	1 teaspoon vanilla
Long-handled spoon	2½ cups milk
Table knife	Nutmeg

1 Heat oven to 350°.

2 Place custard cups in ungreased baking pan. Empty ¼ cup miniature marshmallows into each custard cup.

3 Beat 3 eggs, ⅓ cup sugar, dash of salt and 1 teaspoon vanilla in bowl.

4 Scald 2½ cups milk in saucepan. Gradually stir the scalded milk into the egg mixture.

5 Dip out the custard with a measuring cup and pour about ½ cup into each custard cup. Sprinkle each with a little nutmeg.

6 Ask someone older to pour very hot water into the baking pan to within ½ inch of the tops of the custard cups and to lift the pan into oven.

7 Bake in 350° oven about 45 minutes or until knife inserted halfway between the center and edge of a custard comes out clean.

8 Ask someone older to remove the pan from oven and to lift the custards out of the water. After the custards are cool enough to handle, refrigerate them.

Note: To scald milk, heat it to just below boiling—small bubbles will form in the milk around the edge of the saucepan.

Creamy Orange Tapioca

4 servings.

Utensils	Ingredients
Medium saucepan	¼ cup sugar
Long-handled spoon	2 tablespoons quick-cooking tapioca
Rubber scraper	1¼ cups orange juice
4 dessert dishes	1¼ cups frozen whipped topping, thawed
	4 maraschino cherries (if you like)

1 Mix ¼ cup sugar, 2 tablespoons tapioca and 1¼ cups orange juice in saucepan. Let stand 5 minutes.

2 Heat to boiling over medium-high heat, stirring constantly. Remove from heat. Cool 20 minutes.

3 Stir tapioca mixture with rubber scraper, then fold in 1 cup of the whipped topping.

4 Divide the tapioca mixture among 4 dessert dishes and top each serving with a spoonful of remaining whipped topping and 1 maraschino cherry.

Pound Cake with Pokey Frosting

Utensils	Ingredients
Pastry brush	1 package (16 ounces) golden pound cake mix
Loaf pan, 9 × 5 × 3 inches	
Small mixer bowl	⅔ cup water
Electric mixer	2 eggs
Wooden pick	1 cup powdered sugar
Wire cooling rack	½ teaspoon grated orange peel
Serving plate	
Fork or skewer	½ cup orange juice
Small bowl	

1 Heat oven to 325°. Generously grease loaf pan with shortening, using pastry brush. Sprinkle a little flour into the pan and shake gently from side to side until the flour coats the bottom and sides. Empty out remaining flour.

2 Prepare the pound cake mix as directed on package. After mixing, pour the batter into the greased and floured pan.

3 Bake in 325° oven about 1 hour and 15 minutes or until wooden pick inserted in the center of the cake comes out clean. Cool the cake on rack 10 minutes, then remove from the pan to plate. Poke holes ½ inch apart in the top with fork.

4 Mix 1 cup powdered sugar, ½ teaspoon grated orange peel and ½ cup orange juice in small bowl with fork. Pour a little at a time over the top of the cake.

Angel Food Cake with Snowstorm Frosting

Pictured on the facing page.

Utensils	Ingredients
Serving plate	1 angel food or chiffon cake
Spatula or table knife	1 carton (4 ounces) frozen whipped topping, thawed
	2⅔ cups (two 3½-ounce cans) flaked coconut

1 Place the cake on serving plate. Frost the cake with the whipped topping, using spatula.

2 Sprinkle the cake with 2⅔ cups coconut. Refrigerate until serving time.

Note: You can use tinted coconut if you like.

Rocky Road Frosting

Enough to frost 13 × 9-inch cake.

Utensils	Ingredients
Small saucepan	1 tub (16½ ounces) dark Dutch fudge ready-to-spread frosting
Long-handled spoon	
Spatula	1 cup miniature marshmallows
	½ cup chopped nuts

1 Heat the frosting in saucepan over low heat until frosting is liquid, stirring constantly. Remove from heat.

2 Stir in 1 cup miniature marshmallows and ½ cup chopped nuts. Pour the frosting over a cooled cake (chocolate, yellow or banana are good) and spread with spatula.

Pictured: Angel Food Cake with Snowstorm Frosting (above) and Chocolate Bunnies (page 82), Peanutty Chocolate Pie (page 78) and Big Fat Cookies (page 19)

BEST CAKE

BEST PIE

BEST COOKIES

Milk Chocolate Brownie Cake

Utensils	Ingredients
Pastry brush	1 cup butter or
Jelly roll pan,	margarine (2 sticks)
15½ × 10½ × 1 inch	1 cup water
Large saucepan	⅓ cup cocoa
Long-handled spoon	2 cups all-purpose
Egg beater	flour*
Rubber scraper	2 cups sugar
Wooden pick	1 teaspoon baking soda
Wire cooling rack	½ teaspoon salt
Spatula	2 eggs
	½ cup plain yogurt or
	dairy sour cream
	Cherry Frosting (right)

1 Heat oven to 375°. Grease jelly roll pan with shortening, using pastry brush.

2 Heat 1 cup butter, 1 cup water and ⅓ cup cocoa to boiling in saucepan, stirring occasionally. Remove from heat.

3 Add 2 cups flour, 2 cups sugar, 1 teaspoon baking soda, ½ teaspoon salt, 2 eggs and ½ cup yogurt and beat until smooth. (The batter will be very thin.)

4 Pour the batter into the greased pan.

5 Ask someone to open the oven door for you—that full pan needs 2 hands. Bake in 375° oven 20 to 25 minutes or until wooden pick inserted in the center of the cake comes out clean. Cool the cake on rack.

6 While the cake is cooling, prepare Cherry Frosting. Pour the frosting over the cooled cake and spread with spatula.

* Do not use self-rising flour in this recipe.

Cherry Frosting

Utensils	Ingredients
Kitchen scissors	1 jar (6 ounces)
Large saucepan	maraschino cherries
Long-handled spoon	½ cup butter or
Egg beater	margarine (1 stick)
	⅓ cup cocoa
	⅓ cup milk
	1 package (16 ounces)
	powdered sugar (about
	4½ cups)
	1 teaspoon almond
	extract
	Dash of salt

1 Drain the jar of maraschino cherries. Cut each cherry into 6 pieces with scissors; drain.

2 Heat ½ cup butter, ⅓ cup cocoa and ⅓ cup milk to boiling in saucepan, stirring occasionally. Remove from heat.

3 Add the powdered sugar and beat until smooth.

4 Stir in 1 teaspoon almond extract, dash of salt and the cherry pieces. Now continue with Step 6 of the cake recipe.

Peach Double Deckers

Pictured on page 67.

4 double deckers.

Utensils	Ingredients
2 small bowls	1 package (11 or 22 ounces) pie crust sticks
Fork	
Cookie sheet	2 tablespoons water
Custard cup	1 tablespoon granulated sugar
Spoon	
Pancake turner	½ teaspoon cinnamon
Wire cooling rack	1 can (29 ounces) sliced peaches
Egg beater	
4 dessert plates	½ cup chilled whipping cream
	2 tablespoons powdered sugar
	Nutmeg

1 Heat oven to 475°.

2 Take out 1 pie crust stick. (Save remaining for another time.) Prepare pastry for One-crust Pie as directed on package except —do not roll out. Divide the pastry into 8 equal parts. Shape each into a ball.

3 Pat each ball into a 3½-inch circle on ungreased cookie sheet. Prick each pastry circle with fork at ½-inch intervals, making holes big enough so they won't close up when you bake the circles. (This prevents puffing.)

4 Mix 1 tablespoon granulated sugar and ½ teaspoon cinnamon in custard cup. Sprinkle the pastry circles with the sugar-cinnamon mixture.

5 Bake in 475° oven 7 minutes or until light brown. Lift circles to rack with pancake turner. (These can be baked several hours ahead of time.)

6 Twenty minutes before serving the desserts, refrigerate another small bowl. Just before serving, drain the can of peaches.

7 Beat ½ cup whipping cream and 2 tablespoons powdered sugar in the chilled bowl.

8 Place 1 baked circle on each of 4 dessert plates. Spoon some whipped cream mixture and some peaches onto each. Cover with remaining circles and top with remaining whipped cream mixture and peaches. Sprinkle with nutmeg.

VARIATION

Fruit Double Deckers: Follow recipe for Peach Double Deckers except—in place of the can of sliced peaches, use 1 can (21 ounces) cherry, peach, apple, raisin or mincemeat pie filling. Do not drain the liquid from the can.

Reminder! *Whenever you use an electric mixer, be sure that it's unplugged and turned to "off" before you put the beaters in or take them out. And you wouldn't ever scrape the side of the bowl without turning the mixer off, would you?*

Pink Meringue Pie

Utensils	Ingredients
Table knife	8- or 9-inch frozen
8-inch pie pan	unbaked pie shell
Fork	1 can (21 ounces)
Wire cooling rack	cherry pie filling
Small saucepan	Pink Meringue (right)
Long-handled spoon	
Rubber scraper	

1 Heat oven to temperature given on pie shell package.

2 If using 9-inch frozen pie shell, allow it to stand 5 minutes at room temperature. Loosen with knife, then slide the shell into 8-inch pie pan. Ease the pastry to fit around the edge. (If using 8-inch frozen shell, omit this step.) When you prick the pastry with a fork, make holes large enough so they won't close up when you bake the shell. (This prevents puffing.)

3 Bake the pie shell as directed on package for empty baked crust. Cool on rack.

4 Heat the pie filling in saucepan over low heat 5 to 10 minutes, stirring occasionally. Remove from heat. While the filling is heating, make Pink Meringue.

5 Reduce oven temperature to 400°. Pour the hot pie filling into the pie shell. Spoon the meringue around the edges of the hot pie filling and swirl it with rubber scraper. Be careful to seal the meringue to the edge of the crust to prevent shrinking.

6 Bake in 400° oven about 8 minutes or until the peaks of the meringue are a delicate golden brown. Serve warm or cold.

Pink Meringue

Utensils	Ingredients
Small mixer bowl	3 eggs
Small bowl	¼ teaspoon cream of
Electric mixer	tartar
Rubber scraper	6 tablespoons sugar
	½ teaspoon vanilla
	10 drops red food color

1 Separate the egg whites from the yolks.* Pour the whites into small mixer bowl. Cover the egg yolks tightly in small bowl and refrigerate to use within a day or two.

2 Sprinkle ¼ teaspoon cream of tartar over the egg whites. Beat on high speed until foamy. Gradually beat in 6 tablespoons sugar, ½ teaspoon vanilla and 10 drops red food color.

3 Continue beating until stiff and glossy, about 5 minutes. Turn off the mixer occasionally and scrape the side of the bowl with rubber scraper. Now go back to Step 5 of the pie recipe.

* To separate an egg, you will need 2 bowls. Hold the egg over 1 bowl. Gently crack the shell in the middle with a knife. With the cracked side on top, pull open the shell. Rock the yolk from one shell half to the other until all the white flows into the bowl. Drop the yolk into the second bowl. If a bit of yolk falls into the white, lift it out with a spoon (be sure to get it all out, or the whites won't beat up properly!)

VARIATION

Blue Meringue Pie: Follow recipe for Pink Meringue Pie except—in place of cherry pie filling, use blueberry pie filling. In place of 10 drops red food color, use 4 drops blue food color and 2 drops red food color.

To separate an egg, crack the shell with a knife, then with the cracked side on top, pull it open.

Rock the yolk back and forth between the shell halves until all the white flows into a bowl.

Beat the egg white mixture until it's stiff and glossy— the meringue should stand up in peaks.

Drop the meringue by spoonfuls onto the hot pie filling, then spread it with a rubber scraper.

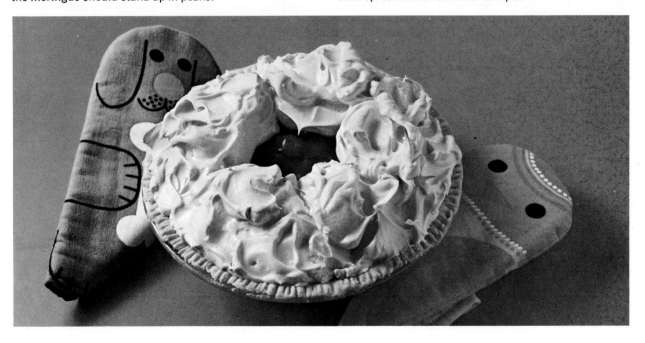

Sherbet Pie in Coconut Crust

Utensils	Ingredients
9-inch pie pan	3 tablespoons butter or
Spoon	margarine, softened
Ice-cream scoop	1½ cups flaked coconut
or large spoon	4 cups lime, raspberry,
	orange or lemon sher-
	bet (or a mixture of
	flavors if you like)

1 Heat oven to 325°. Grease pie pan with 3 tablespoons butter.

2 Press 1½ cups coconut firmly and evenly against the bottom and side of the pan with the back of spoon.

3 Bake in 325° oven 15 to 20 minutes or until golden brown. Cool.

4 Scoop 4 cups sherbet into the cooled crust. Serve right away.

Peanutty Chocolate Pie

Pictured on page 73.

Utensils	Ingredients
Large bowl	1 package (14.3 ounces)
Spoon	chocolate fudge frost-
Cutting board	ing mix
Sharp knife	1 pint (2 cups) chilled
Egg beater	whipping cream
Rubber scraper	Peanut Butter Crumb
	Crust (right)
	½ cup salted peanuts

1 Heat oven to 350°.

2 Mix the chocolate fudge frosting mix

and 1 pint chilled whipping cream in large bowl. Cover the bowl and refrigerate 1 hour.

3 Prepare Peanut Butter Crumb Crust.

4 When the whipping cream mixture has been refrigerated 1 hour, chop ½ cup pea-nuts into tiny pieces on cutting board.

5 Beat the chilled whipping cream mixture until thick and fluffy, about 1 minute. Fold in the chopped peanuts with rubber scraper.

6 Pour into the cooled crust and freeze at least 6 hours or until firm. Spoon on dabs of whipped topping if you like.

Note: Cut skinny slices of this rich pie!

Peanut Butter Crumb Crust

Utensils	Ingredients
Small saucepan	¼ cup butter or mar-
Fork	garine (½ stick)
Spoon	1½ cups packaged
9-inch pie pan	graham cracker
	crumbs
	¼ cup creamy peanut
	butter
	3 tablespoons sugar

1 Heat oven to 350°.

2 Melt ¼ cup butter in saucepan over low heat. Remove from heat. Stir in 1½ cups graham cracker crumbs, ¼ cup peanut butter and 3 tablespoons sugar with fork.

3 Spoon the mixture into pie pan and press firmly and evenly against the bottom and side of the pan with the back of the spoon.

4 Bake in 350° oven 10 minutes. Cool. Now go back to Step 4 of the pie recipe.

Pictured: Cookie Ski Chalet (page 86) and Gumdrop Trees (page 88)

Birthday Ice-Cream Cake

About 12 servings.

Utensils	Ingredients
Shallow pan	½-gallon pail spumoni
Long spatula	(or your favorite
Serving plate	flavor) ice cream
Teaspoon	2½ cups frozen whipped
Candles	topping, thawed
Candle holders	½ cup chocolate caramel
Sharp knife	sauce
Glass	

1 Fill pan almost to the top with warm water.

2 Remove cover from the pail of ice cream. Run spatula around inside of the pail to loosen the ice cream. Dip the pail quickly into the pan of warm water to loosen the ice cream. Place serving plate on top of the pail and turn pail over so the ice cream can slide out onto the plate. Lift off the pail. Place the ice cream in freezer immediately. Freeze about 1 hour or until firm.

3 Frost the ice cream with 2½ cups whipped topping, using the spatula.

4 Drizzle ½ cup chocolate caramel sauce in a circle around the top edge of the cake with teaspoon. Freeze until serving time.

5 Place candles in holders and arrange on top of the cake. Ask someone older for help in lighting the candles. To serve, cut the cake into wedges. (Dip the knife into glass of water for easier cutting.)

Note: In place of the pail of ice cream, you can use a ½-gallon brick of ice cream—just peel off the sides of the carton and lift the block of ice cream to a plate. Frost as directed above. In place of the frozen whipped topping, you can use 1 envelope (about 1½ ounces) dessert topping mix, prepared as directed on envelope.

Bouncing Ball Punch

About 2 quarts punch.

Utensils	Ingredients
Punch bowl	2 packages (16 ounces
Long-handled spoon	each) frozen melon
	balls
	1 can (46 ounces)
	your favorite fruit
	punch drink
	1 can (6 ounces) frozen
	lemonade concentrate
	Water

1 About 40 minutes before you want to serve punch, remove the frozen melon balls from freezer. Let stand at room temperature about 20 minutes for easier opening.

2 Mix the fruit punch drink, lemonade concentrate and two 6-ounce cans water (use the lemonade can) in punch bowl. Add the frozen melon balls and let stand 15 minutes. Stir and serve.

Valentine's Day

No-Cook Divinity

60 to 72 candies.

Utensils	Ingredients
Small saucepan	½ cup water
Small mixer bowl	1 package (7.2 ounces) fluffy white frosting mix
Electric mixer	
Rubber scraper	⅓ cup light corn syrup
Large mixer bowl	1 teaspoon vanilla
Spoon	1 package (16 ounces) powdered sugar (about 4½ cups)
Teaspoon	
Waxed paper	
	1 cup chopped nuts

1 Heat ½ cup water just to boiling in saucepan over medium-high heat. Pour the boiling water into small mixer bowl. Add the frosting mix, ⅓ cup corn syrup and 1 teaspoon vanilla.

2 Beat on high speed until stiff peaks form, about 5 minutes. Turn off the mixer occasionally and scrape the side of the bowl with the rubber scraper.

3 Empty the mixture into large mixer bowl and gradually beat in the powdered sugar on low speed.

4 Stir in 1 cup chopped nuts. Drop the mixture by teaspoonfuls about 1 inch apart onto waxed paper. Let stand until the surface of the candies feels firm, then turn them over and let stand at least 12 hours to dry.

Note: You can store leftover candy in a container with a tight cover at room temperature or freeze in the container as long as 2 months.

Cook's Corner

Why don't you make a Heart Cake for Valentine's Day? Heat the oven to 350°. Grease and flour 1 square baking pan, 8x8x2 inches, and 1 round layer pan, 8x1½ inches. Prepare 1 package (18.5 ounces) white cake mix with pudding as directed except—pour the batter into the pans, making sure both are filled to an equal depth. Bake the layers 30 to 35 minutes or until cake pulls away from sides of pans and springs back when touched lightly in center. Cool the layers as directed.

Place the square layer on a large tray with 1 point toward you. Cut the round layer in half. Place the cut edge of each half against the top edges of the square to make a heart.

Prepare 1 package (7.2 ounces) fluffy white frosting mix as directed and frost the Heart Cake, using a spatula. Decorate the cake or spell out a Valentine message with cinnamon candies, or sprinkle the cake with flaked coconut.

Chocolate Bunnies or Chicks

Pictured on page 73.

About 5 bunnies or chicks.

Utensils	Ingredients
Cookie sheet	1 package (6 ounces)
Waxed paper	semisweet chocolate
Small saucepan	chips
Long-handled spoon	1 tablespoon shortening
Bunny or chick cookie	Tiny colored candies
cutter	

1 Cover cookie sheet with waxed paper.

2 Heat the chocolate chips and 1 tablespoon shortening in saucepan over low heat until chocolate chips melt, stirring constantly.

3 Spread the chocolate mixture in a 6-inch square about ¼ inch thick on the waxed paper. Sprinkle generously with candies. Refrigerate 10 minutes. Cut out chocolate figures with cookie cutter.

4 Refrigerate 30 minutes or until firm. (The cook gets to eat the scraps!)

5 Use bunnies or chicks to decorate a frosted cake or press onto sugar cookies or graham crackers. Or, stick them on with a little dab of ready-to-spread frosting.

Noodle Nests

16 nests.

Utensils	Ingredients
Cookie sheet	1 tub (16½ ounces)
Waxed paper	your favorite flavor
Large saucepan	ready-to-spread
Long-handled spoon	frosting
	4 cups chow mein
	noodles
	Small jelly beans

1 Cover cookie sheet with waxed paper.

2 Heat the frosting in saucepan over low heat until frosting is liquid, stirring occasionally. Remove from heat.

3 Stir in 4 cups chow mein noodles until coated. Drop the mixture by ¼ cupfuls about 1 inch apart onto the waxed paper. Make a hollow in the center of each, using the back of the spoon. Does it look like a nest? Fill with jelly beans (3 to 5 for each nest). Let stand until firm.

Cook's Corner

You can make a nest full of eggs to decorate the top of a cupcake, a large cookie or a round cake. Frost the cupcake, cookie or cake (use ready-to-spread frosting if you like). While the frosting is still sticky, press on some white or pastel-colored coconut and some tiny jelly beans. There—it's springtime!

HALLOWEEN

Little Pumpkin Cups

12 cups.

Utensils	Ingredients
1 or 2 muffin pans	2 envelopes (about 1½
12 paper baking cups	ounces each) whipped
Large mixer bowl	topping mix
Electric mixer	1 cup milk
Rubber scraper	1 teaspoon vanilla
	1 teaspoon cinnamon
	½ teaspoon salt
	¼ teaspoon cloves
	¼ teaspoon ginger
	¼ teaspoon nutmeg
	½ can (16-ounce size)
	pumpkin (about 1
	cup)
	Candy corn

1 Line 12 muffin cups with baking cups. Prepare the topping mix as directed on envelopes, using a total of 1 cup milk and 1 teaspoon vanilla except—add 1 teaspoon cinnamon, ½ teaspoon salt, ¼ teaspoon cloves, ¼ teaspoon ginger and ¼ teaspoon nutmeg before beating. Fold in the pumpkin with rubber scraper.

2 Divide the mixture among the paper-lined muffin cups. Decorate each serving with candy corn. Refrigerate as long as 2 hours or freeze as long as 8 hours and remove to refrigerator 1 hour before serving.

Golden Pumpkin Loaf

Utensils	Ingredients
Pastry brush	1 cup sugar
Loaf pan, 9 × 5 × 3	1 egg
inches	1 can (16 ounces)
Large mixer bowl	pumpkin
Electric mixer	3 cups buttermilk baking
Wooden pick	mix
Wire cooling rack	1 teaspoon pumpkin pie
	spice
	½ teaspoon cloves
	½ teaspoon nutmeg

1 Heat oven to 350°. Generously grease loaf pan with shortening, using pastry brush.

2 Beat 1 cup sugar, 1 egg and the pumpkin in mixer bowl on medium speed 30 seconds. Gradually beat in remaining ingredients on low speed just until smooth. Pour into the greased pan.

3 Bake at 350° 1 hour and 10 minutes or until wooden pick inserted in center comes out clean.

4 Cool the pumpkin loaf 10 minutes on rack, then remove from the pan. Serve warm or cold.

Ghost Cake with Flaming Eyes

Utensils	Ingredients
Pastry brush	1 package (18.5 ounces) yellow cake mix with pudding
Oblong baking pan, 13 × 9 × 2 inches	
Large mixer bowl	1 cup water
Electric mixer	3 eggs
Rubber scraper	⅓ cup salad oil
Wooden picks	1 package (7.2 ounces) fluffy white frosting mix
Wire cooling rack	
Tray, 16 × 12 inches, breadboard or aluminum foil-covered cardboard	1 cup water
	2 sugar cubes
	Licorice string
Ruler	1 teaspoon lemon extract
Small mixer bowl	
Sharp knife	
Spatula	

1 Heat oven to 350°. Generously grease baking pan with shortening, using pastry brush. Sprinkle a little flour into the pan and shake gently from side to side until flour coats the bottom and sides. Empty out remaining flour.

2 Prepare the cake mix as directed on package. (When you break the eggs, crack each in the middle and pour out the egg. Then save the 2 best shell halves. Wash these halves and turn upside down to dry.) After mixing, pour the batter into the greased and floured pan.

3 Bake in 350° oven 35 to 40 minutes or until wooden pick inserted in the center comes out clean. Cool the cake 10 minutes on rack, then remove from the pan to tray.

4 After the cake is cool, measure across one short edge of the cake and mark the center with a wooden pick. Measure 4 inches down each long edge and mark with picks. Prepare the frosting as directed on package.

5 Cut the cake between the center wooden pick and side picks in a curve to make a rounded top for the ghost's head. Slide the cut corners down the sides to about the center of the cake. Turn the corners so the cut sides are up, to make arms that look as if they're reaching out for you. Attach the arms to the sides of the cake with some of the frosting, using spatula.

6 Frost the cake with the spatula. Place the 2 egg shell halves round sides down on cake for eyes. Place 1 sugar cube in each shell half. Make a mouth of licorice string.

7 Just before serving, pour ½ teaspoon lemon extract over each sugar cube. Ask someone older to light them for you. Lights off—it'll be spooky!

Cook's Corner

Bubble, bubble, toil and trouble—stir this brew up on the double! To make a cauldronful of Foaming Witches' Brew, cover the outside of a large kettle with black paper and tape it in place. Or ask someone older to help you scoop out a pumpkin, then line it with aluminum foil. Just before serving, fill the kettle or foil-lined pumpkin with chilled root beer and drop scoops of vanilla ice cream on top. Stir and serve right away. (For less ghostly occasions, pour strawberry-flavored soda pop into a big bowl and drop in scoops of your favorite flavor sherbet.)

Christmas

Cookie Ski Chalet
Pictured on page 79.

Utensils

2 medium bowls
Long-handled spoon
2 cookie sheets
Breadboard and
    pastry cloth
Rolling pin and
    stockinet cover
Custard cup
Ruler
Table knife
Pancake turner
Wire cooling rack
Wooden picks
Cookie cutters
Aluminum foil or tray,
    15 inches across
Brown paper
Spatula
Paintbrush (if you like)
Small bowl
Fork

Ingredients

2 packages (14.5 ounces
    each) gingerbread
    mix
⅓ cup water
⅓ cup more water
2 tubs (16½ ounces
    each) vanilla ready-to-
    spread frosting
Candy-coated chocolate
    candies
1-inch pieces of thick
    licorice
Large marshmallows
¼ cup water
Powdered sugar

1 Mix 1 package gingerbread mix and ⅓ cup water in medium bowl. Mix the second package and ⅓ cup water in another medium bowl. (Do not mix both packages at once.) Cover both bowls and refrigerate at least 2 hours.

2 When the dough has been refrigerated at least 2 hours, heat oven to 375°. Grease cookie sheets with shortening.

3 Cover breadboard with pastry cloth, tucking ends underneath. Cover rolling pin with stockinet cover. For convenience, place some flour in custard cup. Sprinkle the covered board and rolling pin generously with the flour and rub it in until it disappears.

4 Take out 1 bowl of dough. Roll the dough into a rectangle, 14 inches long, 11 inches wide and ¼ inch thick on the covered board. Cut away any uneven edges and save for rerolling.

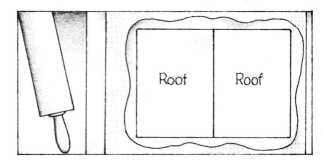

5 Cut the rectangle in half so you have 2 small rectangles, 11 inches long and 7 inches wide. Gently roll the rectangles onto the rolling pin, then lift to a greased cookie sheet and unroll.

6 Bake in 375° oven about 12 minutes. Loosen the rectangles slightly with pancake turner. Let cool 1 to 2 minutes, then carefully slide onto rack.

7 Take out the second bowl of dough. Roll the dough into a rectangle, 15 inches long, 10 inches wide and ¼ inch thick. Cut out a 10-inch square from the rectangle. Lift off the scraps of dough around the square with the pancake turner. (Save the scraps to roll again.)

8 Gently roll the square onto the rolling pin, then lift to the second greased cookie sheet and unroll. Measure 1 edge of the square and make a mark in the center with a wooden pick. Cut from this point to the 2 opposite corners. (If the triangles bake together, recut while warm.)

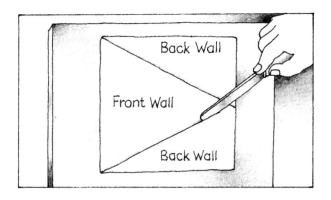

9 Bake in 375° oven about 12 minutes or until the edges are brown. Loosen, cool and remove to the rack as you did before. Cool the walls and roof of your chalet 1 hour.

10 While the walls and roof are cooling, use the scraps to cut out a door, 2½ inches long and 2 inches wide; 2 windows, each 3 inches long and 2½ inches wide; a round window, 1½ inches across; some skis (2 strips of gingerbread, each with a pointed end); and a deer or whatever you like. Bake the skis 6 to 8 minutes and the remaining pieces 8 to 10 minutes. Loosen, cool and

remove to the rack as you did before except—turn up the pointed ends of the skis while they're still warm. Then clean up all the dishes and get ready for the real fun—putting your chalet together.

To Put Your Chalet Together

1 Cover the breadboard with aluminum foil or use a tray.

2 Measure and cut out a rectangle, 9½ inches long and 5½ inches wide, of brown paper. Attach the paper to the middle of the board (or weight it on the tray). Spread some of the frosting from the first tub on the board around the paper with spatula, touching but not covering the edge of the paper, in an outline ¾ inch wide and ¼ inch high. Lift off the paper and throw it away.

3 Spread some frosting on one short (7-inch) edge of each cookie rectangle. Stick these edges together. (They make the peak of the roof.) Press the bottom edges of the rectangles into the frosting on the board. Add extra frosting if you need it to hold the rectangles securely. Now you have the roof of your chalet.

4 Frost all the edges of the biggest cookie triangle. Ease it under the A-frame roof until there is 1 inch of roof overhanging the wall. Press roof gently against the wall to make sure everything is secure.

5 Put the edges of the other 2 triangles together with frosting to make a triangle like the first one, then frost all the edges. Ease under the A-frame roof to complete your chalet. (This may take 4 hands—2 to ease and 2 to hold the roof.) Let stand about 20 minutes so the frosting becomes firm. (If there is a gap at the peak of your roof, cut a piece of cardboard to cover it and frost over the cardboard.)

To Trim Your Chalet

1 Frost the back side of each door and window and press them onto the outside of the walls (the door and 2 windows go in front, and 1 window goes in back). Let stand 10 minutes, then "paint" on window panes with a wooden pick or paintbrush dipped in frosting. Stick decorations on with dabs of frosting. Here's a suggestion: candy-coated chocolate candies around the windows and licorice under the overhanging roof (see picture) for beams.

2 Spread remaining frosting from the first tub on the board to make snow. Stick large marshmallows in it for hills. Lean the skis against the walls of the chalet and stand other cookie figures in the frosting if you like. (You can outline the skis with a wooden pick dipped in frosting if you like.)

3 Empty the second tub of frosting into small bowl. Stir in ¼ cup water with fork. Frost the roof and marshmallow hills. Sprinkle some powdered sugar over the snow.

Try this cookie house as a team project for the entire family. It's much more fun, and you'll have lots of hands to help fit it together.

If the weather is very damp when you make your ski chalet, bake the walls and roof a few minutes longer than the recipe calls for. Then store the cookie pieces overnight in the turned-off (cool) oven. This will keep them from picking up any dampness from the air and getting soggy.

Gumdrop Trees

Pictured on page 79.

6 trees.

Utensils	Ingredients
Cookie sheet	4 cups toasted oat cereal
Large bowl	
Large saucepan	32 large marshmallows or 3 cups miniature marshmallows
Long-handled spoon	
Kitchen scissors	
Glass	3 tablespoons butter or margarine
	½ teaspoon vanilla
	½ teaspoon green food color
	Small gumdrops

1 Grease cookie sheet with some butter or margarine.

2 Empty 4 cups cereal into bowl.

3 Heat 32 large marshmallows and 3 tablespoons butter in saucepan over medium heat until the marshmallows melt. Stir until smooth. Remove from heat. Stir in ½ teaspoon vanilla and ½ teaspoon food color.

4 Pour the marshmallow mixture over the cereal and stir until the cereal is coated.

5 Rub some butter on your hands and divide the cereal mixture into 6 parts on the greased cookie sheet, using about ⅔ cup for each. Shape each part into a tree shape.

6 Cut the gumdrops into slices with scissors. (Dip the scissors into glass of water to keep the candy from sticking.) Press the gumdrop slices onto the trees.

Gifts from the Kitchen

Creamy Caramels

Pictured on page 90.

64 caramel squares.

Utensils	Ingredients
Square baking pan, 8 × 8 × 2 inches	1 package (14.3 ounces) butter pecan frosting mix
Medium saucepan	½ cup butter or margarine (1 stick)
Long-handled spoon	
Candy thermometer	1 cup half-and-half
Glass	½ cup light corn syrup
Sharp knife	

1 Grease baking pan with some butter or margarine.

2 Mix the frosting mix, ½ cup butter, 1 cup half-and-half and ½ cup corn syrup in saucepan, stirring until just blended.

3 Cook without stirring over medium heat to 256° on candy thermometer or until a small amount of the mixture dropped into glass of very cold water forms a hard ball, about 30 minutes. Pour the mixture into the buttered pan. Refrigerate about 1 hour or until firm. Cut into 1-inch squares.

Homemade Crunchy Peanut Butter

1 cup peanut butter.

Utensils	Ingredients
Blender	2 cans (6½ ounces each) salted peanuts (2½ cups)
Rubber scraper	
Small bowl or jar	
	2 tablespoons butter or margarine, softened

1 Measure ½ cup of the peanuts. (You'll use them later.) Empty remaining peanuts (2 cups) into blender container. Cover and blend on low speed 10 seconds or until the peanuts are chopped.

2 Add 2 tablespoons butter to the chopped peanuts. Cover and blend on low speed 10 seconds. Turn off the blender, uncover and scrape down the sides with rubber scraper.

3 Cover and blend on low speed 5 seconds. Turn off the blender, uncover and scrape down the sides again. Repeat this step 3 or 4 times or until the peanut butter starts to get smooth. Cover and blend on highest speed 1 minute.

4 Uncover and add the ½ cup peanuts. Cover and blend on medium speed 3 seconds.

5 Empty the peanut butter into bowl. Refrigerate about 30 minutes.

VARIATION

Smooth Peanut Butter: Blend all 2½ cups peanuts in step 1. Then continue as above except—leave out step 4.

Caramel Apples

Pictured on the facing page.

6 apples.

Utensils	Ingredients
6 wooden ice-cream sticks	6 medium apples
Waxed paper	6 tablespoons granola or chopped salted peanuts
Double boiler or medium saucepan	1 package (14 ounces) vanilla caramels
Long-handled spoon	3 tablespoons water
	¼ cup creamy peanut butter
	½ teaspoon cinnamon

1 Wash 6 apples and poke an ice-cream stick in the stem end of each.

2 Using 1 tablespoon of granola for each mound, make 6 mounds of granola about 3 inches apart on waxed paper.

3 Heat the caramels, 3 tablespoons water, ¼ cup peanut butter and ½ teaspoon cinnamon in top of double boiler over hot water until caramels melt and the mixture is smooth, about 20 minutes, stirring frequently.

4 Remove from heat. (Keep the top of the double boiler over the hot water.)

5 Dip each apple in the hot caramel mixture and spoon mixture over the apple until it is completely coated. Hold the apple right side up by the stick for a second, then place it stick side up on one of the mounds of granola. Turn the apple so all the granola sticks to it.

6 Refrigerate about 1 hour or until the caramel coating is firm.

Pictured: Rosy Grape Jelly, Gumdrop Squares, Caramel Apple, Frosted Pretzels, Creamy Caramels, Rocky Road Fudge, Peppermint Taffy (pages 89-93)

Gumdrop Squares

Pictured on the facing page.

About 45 squares.

Utensils	Ingredients
Medium saucepan	1⅓ cups applesauce
Long-handled spoon	2 envelopes unflavored gelatin
Loaf pan, 9 × 5 × 3 inches	1 package (6 ounces) your favorite fruit-flavored gelatin
Rubber scraper	2 cups sugar
Table knife	1 teaspoon bottled lemon juice
Glass	Sugar
Cookie sheet	
Small bowl	

1 Mix 1⅓ cups applesauce, the unflavored gelatin, fruit-flavored gelatin, 2 cups sugar and 1 teaspoon lemon juice in saucepan. Heat to boiling and boil 1 minute, stirring frequently.

2 Fill loaf pan halfway to the top with cold water. Pour the water out, then immediately pour the gelatin mixture into the wet pan, using rubber scraper to clean the side of the saucepan.

3 When the loaf pan is cool enough to touch, refrigerate about 3 hours or until the candy is firm.

4 Cut the candy into 1-inch squares. (Dip the knife in glass of water to keep the candy from sticking.)

5 Lift each square from the pan onto ungreased cookie sheet. Let stand at least 8 hours to dry.

6 After the candy has dried, place some sugar in bowl, then roll each square in the sugar until all sides are coated.

Peppermint Taffy

Pictured on page 90.

About 1 pound taffy.

Utensils	Ingredients
2 square baking pans, 8 × 8 × 2 inches	1 cup sugar
	¾ cup light corn syrup
Medium saucepan	⅔ cup water
Long-handled spoon	1 tablespoon cornstarch
Candy thermometer	2 tablespoons butter or margarine
Glass	
Kitchen scissors	1 teaspoon salt
Plastic wrap	1 tablespoon peppermint extract
	8 to 10 drops red food color

1 Grease baking pans with some butter or margarine.

2 Heat all ingredients except the peppermint extract and food color just to boiling in saucepan over medium heat, stirring constantly. Cook without stirring to 256° on candy thermometer or until a small amount of the mixture dropped into glass of very cold water forms a hard ball, about 30 minutes.

3 Remove from heat and stir in 1 tablespoon peppermint extract. Pour half the mixture into one of the buttered pans. Stir 8 to 10 drops food color into remaining mixture, then pour into the other buttered pan. Let cool 15 to 20 minutes. (Ask for help from someone older in deciding when the taffy is cool enough to pull—it has to be cooled in the center and not just at the edges.)

4 When the taffy is ready to pull, wash and dry your hands and rub some butter on them.

5 Keep the 2 colors of taffy separate. Fold, double and pull each color of taffy until it is light in color and stiff. (Ask a brother, sister or friend to help.) If the taffy sticks, rub some more butter on your hands.

6 Pull each color of taffy into a long strip ½ inch wide, then put the 2 colors together and twist. Cut into 1- to 3-inch pieces with scissors. Shape the longer pieces into candy canes. (If the taffy becomes too hard to pull, heat it in a 350° oven a few minutes to soften it.)

7 Wrap each piece with plastic wrap. (Taffy will lose its shape if it isn't wrapped.)

Frosted Pretzels

Pictured on page 90.

15 pretzels.

Utensils	Ingredients
Rubber scraper	1 tub (16½ ounces) vanilla ready-to-spread frosting
Double boiler	
Long-handled spoon	
Waxed paper	15 pretzel twists

1 Measure 1 cup frosting. (Refrigerate remaining frosting for another time.)

2 Heat the 1 cup frosting in top of double boiler over hot water until frosting is liquid, stirring occasionally. Remove from heat. (Keep the top of the double boiler over the hot water.)

3 Dip 15 pretzel twists into the frosting with your fingers, then place them on waxed paper. Let dry 8 hours.

Rosy Grape Jelly

Pictured on page 90.

5 jars jelly.

Utensils	Ingredients
Five 7-ounce jars or glasses	2 cups cranberry juice
Kitchen towel	¾ cup grape juice
4-quart saucepan	1 package (1¾ ounces) powdered fruit pectin
Long-handled spoon	3¼ cups sugar
Jar lids or aluminum foil	

1 Wash jars in hot, soapy water. Rinse thoroughly and turn upside down on folded towel to drain. (The jars should be warm and dry when you fill them with jelly.)

2 Mix thoroughly 2 cups cranberry juice, ¾ cup grape juice and the pectin in saucepan. (There shouldn't be any lumps.) Heat to boiling over high heat, stirring constantly. Stir in 3¼ cups sugar all at once. Heat to boiling and boil 1 minute, stirring constantly.

3 Remove from heat and quickly skim off any bubbles. Ask someone older to pour the jelly into the jars for you, since it's very hot. (This should be done right away.)

4 Let jars stand 1 hour, then cover with lids. Refrigerate. (The jelly will keep as long as 3 weeks in the refrigerator or as long as 6 months in the freezer. To thaw frozen jelly, refrigerate or let stand at room temperature several hours.)

Note: This recipe will also fill seven 5-ounce glasses or eight 4½-ounce baby food jars. Any size or shape dishwasher-safe containers made of glass or plastic can be used.

Cook's Corner

Have you ever thought of giving homemade food gifts to your family and friends? They're very special presents because you make them yourself.

Part of the fun of making jelly is eating it—and another part is giving it away. When you give a jar as a present, it's nice to paste on a label you've made. Wrap the jar with bright tissue paper or a scrap of colorful cloth and fasten it with yarn or ribbon. Include a tag with instructions on how to store the jelly if you like.

Rocky Road Fudge

Pictured on page 90.

64 fudge squares.

Utensils	Ingredients
Square baking pan, 8 × 8 × 2 inches	¼ cup milk
Medium saucepan	1 package (11½ ounces) milk chocolate chips
Long-handled spoon	2 cups miniature marshmallows
Spatula	½ cup chopped nuts
Table knife	Dash of salt

1 Grease baking pan with some butter or margarine.

2 Heat ¼ cup milk and the chocolate chips in saucepan over low heat until chocolate chips melt, stirring constantly.

3 Remove from heat. Stir in 2 cups miniature marshmallows, ½ cup chopped nuts and dash of salt. (The marshmallows will make little lumps in the candy.)

4 Spread the candy in the buttered pan with spatula. Refrigerate about 1 hour or until firm. Cut into 1-inch squares.

INDEX